Tears Turned

to Gold

A Survivor's Story

Miss Brenda,
    Thank you for your
faithful care of our children
each day on the bus.
            - Marie Morrow

By Marie Morrow

Tears Turned to Gold

Copyright © 2013 Marie Morrow

Cover design by: Christa Publishing
Interior layout by Dave Reed
Photography by Daniel Morrow

ISBN-10: 0-9892506-0-1

ISBN-13: 978-0-9892506-0-3

To see more from this author visit: MariesReflections.com

To leave feedback or contact this author, please email:

contact@mariesreflections.com

Note: All Bible scriptures used in this book are taken from the New International Version unless otherwise noted. King James Version is noted as KJV.

Printed in U.S.A

Dedication

This book is dedicated to those who are
facing the pains and hardships of life. I pray
my story can give you courage and hope to
strengthen you in your journey.

Acknowledgements

This book would not have come to be were it not for my loving husband, Daniel, his faith in me, support, patience, and encouragement. He has stayed by me through thick and thin, lifted me up when I could not stand, and truly been God's greatest blessing in my life. I tell our story with deepest gratitude for the path that we have shared.

I wish to acknowledge my mother, Esther, who worked tirelessly behind the scenes, typing, editing, proofing, helping me and caring for my children while I worked on this book. This major undertaking would not have been possible without her dedication and effort.

I want to thank my sister, Jenna, who sacrificially cared for me and my children during my cancer recovery, and Daniel's mother, who came to our rescue whenever we needed it most.

Special mention is also needed of a dear friend, Nicole Costello, who lovingly and diligently taught and cared for my children every day for two years. I could not have made it without her through that time of illness. Her love, dedication, and fun personality will forever be treasured in my children's memories.

I would like to offer my heartfelt appreciation to those who upheld us in prayer, cared for us when we were sick, and reached out a hand of support and understanding in our times of need. We are forever grateful. I hope that as you read this story, you may see how God brought about the answers to your prayers, and also take part in the blessings which we have received.

Tears Turned to Gold

A Survivor's Story

Table of Contents

INTRODUCTION

This is the story of a young couple and their long and difficult journey down the road of affliction. This is a story of tribulation and triumph, harrowing experiences and supernatural joys. This is a story of faith and perseverance. This is our story.

My name is Marie Morrow. My husband, Daniel, and I have been blessed with four beautiful children. Over the last seven years we have faced many difficult challenges. After some wonderful years in missionary work in Brazil, Japan and Taiwan, we returned to the U.S. to get medical help for my husband. For several years we rode the medical roller coaster as Daniel battled a life-threatening tumor.

Then I fought my own battle with cancer and afterward developed fibromyalgia, a chronic, painful and disabling condition which I have struggled with for five years now, often leaving me bed-ridden and wheelchair bound. Daniel's tumor, though no longer life-threatening for the present, continues to pose a challenge, causing pain and discomfort.

When facing a difficult illness, in addition to the physical strains of pain, fatigue, and other symptoms, there is a vast array of psychological and emotional challenges, such as fear, uncertainty, discouragement, hopelessness, and depression—just to name a few. But for every battle, there can be a victory. For every pain, there can be relief. For every fear, there can be peace. For every sorrow, God will give us His comfort.

This is the story of a relationship—a relationship with God that is alive and intimate. This is not a silent God who lives far away in the clouds somewhere, nor is He confined within the walls of a church. *He is a* God of love, who cares for and is personally involved in the lives of His children.

This is a story of messages—messages of hope, faith, encouragement and guidance received from the Heavenly realm. There is nothing more valuable to me in the whole world than to receive a message of divine guidance and encouragement in times of deep crisis. Jesus still speaks to us today, and His voice is so real.

To write this story and not include these messages we received from Heaven would be to paint a picture with no colors or write a song with no notes. Many times Heaven sees things so differently than we do. God's Word says that *our present sufferings are not worth comparing with the glory that will be revealed in us* (Romans 8:18).

Our story is a journey through many ups and downs, with amazing twists and turns. I have endeavored to tell the full story, both the good and bad, so that you may know that no matter how difficult or unbearable your circumstances are, God's love is strong enough to overcome them. His miracles of help and comfort contrast even more brightly against the darkness of our severest trials.

We have been richly blessed in our lives, as God has poured out His grace and faith sufficiently to meet our many needs. Some of life's purest treasures are mined in the caves of affliction. Precious gems are not formed in the sunshine. Those jewels of greatest value are found in the deep, dark places of the earth. So it has been in our own lives.

God does not place us in those hard, dark places to abandon us. He has faith in us, and with His help, we retrieve the rarest treasures. And when we come into the light again, we bring with us the priceless "*treasures of darkness*" (Isaiah 45:3).

In this book we hope to share with you the many treasures we have gained from our journeys through our caves of affliction. *"He comforts us in all our troubles so that we can comfort those in any trouble, with the comfort we ourselves have received from God"* (2Corinthians 1:4).

Some subjects in this book are of a very personal nature, and have been difficult for me to write about. But these are very real struggles that many people go through, so I hope that in confiding my own experience with you, it may be a help to others who are, perhaps, also facing life's toughest challenges.

This book also contains a number of supernatural experiences and visions, which have been a tremendous encouragement to me during my hours of deepest trial. At first I was hesitant to write about these experiences. I wondered if people would even believe me. But these treasures, which have been such a help to me, are too wonderful to keep to myself. They must be shared.

God has blessed us so richly with the treasures of the spirit that our physical suffering pales by comparison. Surely He did not intend for such wealth to be for us alone. He loves and cares for you just as much. He came that you might have life, and He wants you to live it to the full (John 10:10b). This is the abundant life of the spirit that he gives even when our flesh fails us.

I pray that the comfort we have received in our times of trouble may be a blessing to you also, as you study these treasures of comfort, our Tears Turned to Gold.

Don't miss the thrilling Epilogue, where the story concludes with the great miracles God has done for us. He has brought us out of the fire and water, into a place of rich blessings (Psalm 66:12). Remember, no matter how long the night of your suffering may seem to be, the morning will surely come again. *"Weeping may remain for a night, but rejoicing comes in the morning"* (Psalms 30:5).

Note: All Bible scriptures used in this book are taken from the New International Version unless otherwise noted. King James Version is noted as KJV.

Chapter One

THE HOURGLASS

I knew of his condition when I married him. The benign, slow growing tumor which posed no immediate danger would someday play a major role in our lives. Whether it was my optimistic personality or youthful shortsightedness, I had no fears or doubts about the future. I never really thought about what it might actually mean for us nor could I have possibly imagined what the future had in store.

If I had known from the beginning the wild road that lay ahead, would I still have married him? Absolutely! I have been blest to share this road with a man so wonderful, that no matter how short a time, I would not trade these years for anything in the world. Our journey has taken us to depths and heights I never knew existed.

Several years into our marriage it gradually became more apparent the severity of what we were dealing with. We tried not to think about it, but at times it would sink deep into my consciousness that my time with Daniel might be limited. Slowly choking out his air, this tumor was like an hourglass, counting down the uncertain hours we had together. *How much time did we have left, two years, three, or would it be more?* I found myself asking. *Would he be here to watch our children grow up?*

The feeling that would settle over me was bitter-sweet which seemed only to make our time together more precious to me. I vowed to savor every moment and capture every memory we shared. This influenced the way I viewed life on a number of levels. I saw each of our young children as an extension of our love, his gifts to me, a part of him which I would be able to keep even if he was gone. I promised myself that I would cherish and raise those children as he would want. This would be my gift to him.

For the most part though, I lived in the moment, blocking such thoughts far from my mind, while we talked about grandkids and growing old together. Life was good to us and we lived it well.—Until eventually fate caught up with us.

The tumor was becoming a serious problem. Daniel was growing weaker and finding it more difficult to get up in the morning. His long nights struggling to breathe were taking their toll. On the outside everything seemed fine. Even many of our friends knew nothing of his serious condition.

We were living a happy and fulfilling life as missionaries in Taiwan. We had been there almost three years, and we loved it. This had been the happiest time in our lives. Our work was thriving and our children were happy. God had truly blessed us with many wonderful days. But now everything had to change. While the doctors in Taiwan were skilled professionals, they did not have the advanced medical equipment needed to treat Daniel's serious condition. He would have to go back to the U.S. to see what could be done.

I waited at our home in Taiwan with our three small children and held my breath for four long, agonizing weeks while my husband returned to the U.S., going from specialist to specialist, having tests, tests, and more tests. Things went from bad to worse as the doctors gave their prognosis. They were clear that without immediate treatment, he might not even live a few months. Yet... the treatment itself could kill him.

Over the years, Daniel had seen a number of doctors who each said the same thing: "The tumor (a rare venous-type hemangioma) is benign and will continue to grow and spread very slowly. Any surgery or treatment for it would be extremely dangerous, even life-threatening. So don't put yourself at risk until the tumor itself poses a greater threat. Leave it alone as long as you possibly can."

Knowing the risks of treatment, Daniel had tried hard to ignore the seriousness of his condition. He could feel the toll it was taking on him. He could hardly get out of bed before 11:00 a.m. or later. He was exhausted all the time and the pain and pressure were getting worse. I watched him as he slept fighting desperately for every breath, straining for up to a minute at a time just to get one or two breaths in. His body jerked so hard with the effort, it would shake the whole bed. Daniel had struggled nightly with sleep apnea for years because of the tumor, but now it was so much worse.

As the tumor advanced, spreading from his throat further up into his head, the effects became harder to ignore. Physical strain would easily aggravate his condition, increasing the pain and pressure, clouding his vision, hearing, and mental clarity. He had lived with the weight and burden of his tumor for so long it was a part of his life, and he tried hard to ignore it. He was well aware of the long and painful nightmare that would follow once he started treatment, as well as the serious risks involved. This was a very real fear to him. But now we knew that the time had come. We had no choice but to face our fears head-on.

While we began making arrangements to move our family to Houston, I kept up a brave front. "Everything's going to be fine," I reasoned to myself. "God won't let him die. After all, we're serving Him, doing His will. He would never let something like that happen to *us*." For years I had known that my time with Daniel might be limited, but now as the thought stared me in the face, I refused to believe it.

How quickly that would change, when one day shocking news came about a woman we had known. Colleen was a longtime missionary in Taiwan I had known since I was a child. A great woman and a faithful mother, she was always dedicated to the service of others. She had recently been fighting a long battle with cancer. Last I had heard she was responding to treatment and was recovering. Now the news hit me so suddenly, Colleen had passed away.

This pierced me like a bullet to my heart, affecting me very deeply. Although I knew she was now safe in Heaven, free of the pain and suffering, and had gone on to receive a well deserved reward, yet I found myself overwhelmed with grief and fear. The reality had hit me too close to home. "This really could happen to us *too*." No matter how strong of a faith I claimed to have, I knew then that we are not immune to the tragedy in the world. I felt as though my whole world was falling apart, and fear gripped my heart. Was our hourglass indeed running out?!

A Voice in the Stillness

I wrestled with inward turmoil as I struggled to make sense of what was happening. Where was God when I needed Him? Would He not intervene? Did He care? Through the dark, lonely hours of the night I pleaded my cause in prayer, petitioning for my husband's life, demanding that God not take him from me.

I do not know how long I prayed that night but somehow, when depleted of words and tears, exhausted and empty, my trembling heart was finally quiet enough to listen. It was then that I heard it... the gentle voice breaking through the stillness. I recognized it immediately, the presence was unmistakable. It was the voice of Jesus, strong and compassionate. The very air about me was filled with peace and covered me like a warm blanket. I could feel God's love around me so tangible. As His words spoke to my heart, I felt my fears slowly melt away, one by one.

I'm sure there are skeptics in the crowd ready to close the book right here, thinking this is just wishful fiction. There are those who do not believe that God is real or don't believe that He still speaks to us today. To them I say, bear with me a little longer. Hear out my story in full and then see what your heart tells you. I'll tell you up front, I do not claim to be a saint, a prophet, a psychic or a medium, or to possess any unusual spiritual powers. Nor do I have any title of authority by which to make such a bold claim. My only claim is this, in my hour of need I called out to God and He, in His love and mercy, answered me.

Yet the answer that came was so different from what I had expected. I suddenly found myself seeing things from a whole new perspective. I'd started the night with many fears — for my husband, my children, and myself.

I had wanted God's assurance that He would not take Daniel away from me. But instead I was confronted with a question that touched me in the core of my being. Could I have faith to trust in His loving hand to guide, hold, love and protect us, even if I did not know what the final outcome would be? Who was I to tell Him how He could— or could not—do things? If I truly believe that He is God, and He is love, could I not also trust this love to do me no wrong? This surrender was very painful for me, but when I had determined in my heart to trust Him, no matter what, a great peace filled my soul! As the first light of morning made its way into my room, the heavenly voice warmed its way into my heart and I smiled a sigh of relief. God was with me; there was no room for fear.

"I have always held you, supported you, been there for you and led you beside the still waters. I would never abandon you in any circumstance or in any situation. If you can trust Me with your life, can you not also trust Me with your death?—And know that you are within My strong, loving hands, and that I would never do you any wrong?

"Why do you fear? Why do you cry? Your children are My children. I have created them, carried them, and will keep them through to the end. Each one's life is within My hand and plan. Your needs are before My face. Your tears fill My eyes. Nothing is left to fate or happenstance. Nothing is taken lightly in My eyes.

"I do not play with your hearts and lives. When I do not heal and deliver, it is not because I don't care or get involved. I don't leave you to fight alone, but I carry you through, that, in leaning on Me, you will find your strength—strength to fight, strength to trust, and strength to grow. This love and trust in Me is so beautiful in My eyes!

"I wish to guide you every day in the ways of trust. And as the days get harder, you will cling to Me tighter, till you can trust your whole self to Me and say, "It is not I that live, but Christ that lives within Me" (Galatians 2:20).

"These things will make you strong, and be as a beautiful fragrance upon you. Don't fear the hand that crushes, for, in all tenderness, it will hold and remold. Your children are not left out of the picture. I would do them no wrong. I will meet every need and hear every cry. Nothing will happen to you that would be bad for your children. I hold each dear one in the center of My hand. I do all things well."

I wrote down each precious word as I received it. I clung tightly to them, and found renewed courage to face the fears before me. This heavenly voice would grow to be my frequent companion as we embarked on our seven year long journey of afflictions. It has been my source of strength, without which this book would have no story.

A Difficult Road

News from the doctors was worse than any of us could have expected. The doctors were now suggesting a long road of unimaginably painful and dangerous surgeries and treatments. First he was told that he would need a major surgery—which, in order to remove the wide-spread growth, would involve actually sawing his jaw in half, removing the left side, and reconstructing it with parts from other places on his body. If he survived the surgery, it would take six months to a year to learn to eat and talk again. That is, if he could ever talk again. A large part of his tongue would be removed, and he would likely lose his voice. He would also need to breathe out of a tube in his neck. And after all that, the tumor would still likely grow back again within a few years.

How do you react to something like that?! I was in shock finding all this out through our nightly e-mail communications. I could only imagine how Daniel was taking it. I felt so bad that I couldn't be there in person to comfort and support him. We were half a world apart, yet somehow we would face this together.

After further tests and consultations the doctors determined that surgery would not be an option. Due to the high concentration of blood vessels within the tumor, any kind surgical procedure would result in uncontrolled bleeding, and would most likely be fatal. I must admit I was very relieved when the doctors decided that a different treatment approach was needed. Treatments instead would be aimed at shrinking it a little at a time, just enough to keep it under control. Although less dangerous than the surgery, the procedure would still be risky. Doctors wanted him to begin immediately.

The decision to leave Taiwan was a very sad one for us. We had been so happy there, had many friends, and a wonderful ministry. We had greatly enjoyed living and working together with my brother and his family. But the pain we felt now was more than sadness of what we were losing, it was a greater fear of what we were facing. We were leaving our bit of Heaven on earth to enter a world of hospitals and suffering.

We knew this would be a very difficult time, and had many fears about the road ahead of us. We held tightly onto our faith for the strength we needed to make it through. God, in His mercy and love spoke clearly to us, giving us marvelous words of comfort and encouragement to hold onto in our time of need. He spoke to my heart:

"I will lead you, and be your guide. When the way is rocky, I will give you My hand. When the water is deep, I will lift you up. When the desert is dry, I will give you drink. I will take you through a plain path to a cool stream. I will carry you through."

"How much better it would be if God would just heal Daniel miraculously," we couldn't help but ask. "Then we could be free to fully serve Him. Wouldn't that be a wonderful sample of God's love and power?" We know God has power to heal. We have seen it before.

But, as we learned, there are also times when He chooses not to heal. Instead, He carries us through the storm. And this sample of faith and endurance, joy in the midst of sorrow, and peace which is beyond all understanding, can sometimes reveal God's love and power in unexpected, deeper and richer ways. He says, "When you pass through the waters, I will be with you (Isaiah 43:2)." He told me...

"Faith is not only trusting Me when everything goes well, but the most beautiful and powerful kind of faith is trusting Me when everything isn't going well. When the ship of your life is sailing through storms and raging seas, it's faith that keeps you afloat. It's a faith that will trust no matter what, whether or not I heal you in a miraculous, instant way. Your faith in Me is what is sustaining you and has made Me so very proud of you."

With three small kids, packing and luggage, moving out of a house, selling the car, traveling, etc, I was unable to bring our family back to Houston by myself. Daniel wanted to come back to Taiwan first to help us all make the move together. The doctor warned him that if he did so, he might not live long enough to make it back to the U.S.

Yet Daniel was determined. We had received a specific promise from God for safekeeping on this trip and full assurance in our hearts that Daniel's return was the right thing to do. Little did I realize then how much I would need him, as our little family was about to be caught in the middle of a catastrophic disaster...

Chapter Two

When the Earth Shakes

Only one week after Daniel's return to Taiwan, in the midst of our busy preparation...

Disaster strikes! It's 1:37 a.m., September 21, 1999. A 7.6 magnitude earthquake rocked the island. It was the strongest quake in Taiwan's history. The final death toll exceeded 2,400, with over 11,000 injured. More than 100,000 people were left homeless. Our home was near the epicenter.

Something startled me awake. There was a strange eerie silence. Then the shaking started. It felt like a gentle rocking at first; then it got stronger. Within seconds our house was being jerked from side to side, then in a circular movement; then the whole house seemed to lift up and drop down, and back and forth.

The electricity went out. From the blackness we heard the sounds of shattering glass and everything in the room crashing around us. It was impossible to get out of the house. When we attempted to get up we would be thrown right back down. The force was incredible.

I was able to make my way to my youngest daughter's bed and held her close, praying desperately. Between being half asleep and half in shock I did not think about the giant, wobbly bookcase towering above us. Heavy toy boxes, shelves full of books, and a glass coffee pot were precariously poised over our heads.

The house continued to shake violently. Drawers came out of the dressers. Dishes in the kitchen cupboards were thrown across the dining room. Cupboards, shelves, plant pots and television, all came crashing down. Yet that large book case standing above us was being held by one of God's own angels. Not one thing fell from it; even a cup of water sitting on the shelf did not spill.

My brother's children were in the room above us. Their parents could not get in to them because of the strength of the quake. A large shelf was attached to the wall above their bed. Toys, books and heavy boxes all came down on top of them. Yet, as if protected by an unseen force field, not one thing hit them. When I returned to the house later I noticed their bed littered with the fallen objects, except for the two blank spaces where their little bodies had slept, safe and untouched.

The initial tremor lasted one minute and 40 seconds. It seemed like forever. I was dazed and shocked. During the two years we'd lived in Taiwan I had not felt the slightest tremor nor had I even realized that we were in an earthquake zone. This was so totally unexpected.

After the initial quake we grabbed the kids and hurried to get out of the building. We carried them down the stairs in the dark. Glass crunched beneath our bare feet as we made our way out, but we did not get a single cut. As the first aftershock hit, we climbed over the mess of fallen objects and furniture that only moments before had been our living room and made it outside safely, dressed only in our nightclothes.

Surrounded by buildings, it was just as dangerous on the street, so we took refuge in a small clearing at one end of the housing complex, with about 60 other people. The aftershocks came every two to five minutes—some almost as strong as the quake itself. We could hear the crashing and shattering sounds from the houses around us.

Someone came running to tell us that one of the apartment buildings in our complex had fallen. Later, in morning's light, we were able to see that the first floors had collapsed into the basement below, and the entire building was leaning over, held up by the building next to it, trapping families in the lower floors. Everyone was so scared! Some of our neighbors were crying. We comforted them, held them, and prayed for them.

At first the children were scared. My two-year-old clung to me tightly as the aftershocks rocked us again. I told them that the angels are protecting us, and prayed for them not to be afraid. An amazing peace came over them. My toddler let go of me and began dancing around, singing, "The angels are protecting us. The angels are protecting us." Our neighbors were amazed to see her so happy and peaceful in the middle of such a frightening situation.

Do angels drive? What happened next made me wonder. Daniel and Aaron decided to try to get our cars out of the underground parking lot before it was too late. We would need them to evacuate. Daniel found our car safe and untouched. Aaron's car, though, was not where he parked it. It had moved out of its parking place and rolled across the driveway. The roof above where his car should have been had caved in, yet his car was unscratched. Both cars were brought out safely.

At about 5:00 a.m., we moved to a nearby open field where hundreds of people were gathering. My husband and my brother returned cautiously to the house we shared to get our tents, valuables and a few supplies. Shortly afterwards our complex was blocked off, as fears rose that the damaged buildings nearby could fall.

With our family out of immediate danger, our concern turned toward friends in the city. Daniel and Aaron went to check on friends nearby. It took them an hour to cover even a short distance into town. Flat stretches of road had buckled up into small hills. Large cracks in some areas made the roads impassable for cars. Our motorbike was the only transportation possible, often needing to be carried across the cracks or over debris.

By afternoon everyone from our neighborhood was being evacuated to a nearby military base. About 3,000 people soon joined us there. Day and night the trucks rolled in, bringing evacuees from the surrounding areas. Helicopters brought in those that had been trapped in the mountain villages, where the roads had all been destroyed.

We were busy night and day, setting up tents for people in need, counseling, comforting and praying with those who had lost everything, even loved ones, in the devastating quake.

The Aftermath

"Just ride it like a roller-coaster." I told the kids each time another aftershock came. In our tents out in the open, we were not in any danger from the quakes. Yet after experiencing the big one, every tremor had a way of making your heart jump. I was also aware of the serious effects such aftershocks would have on damaged buildings where rescue operations were underway. But for the children's sake I tried to make a game out of it. "Woahhh!" We'd all say together, as if on an amusement ride, while being jostled from side to side again. There were reported to be over 10,000 aftershocks in the two weeks following the quake.

Life in the camp was quite a circus. We were living in tents with our three small kids, alongside my brother, Aaron, and his wife, Iona, and their three kids. Besides keeping our own children occupied, we often found ourselves entertaining the crowds of children that surrounded us. If I wanted to give my kids a story, I had 40 children who wanted one too. If I pulled out coloring books, I needed 30 more. As the only foreigners at the camp, and a family with so many blond children, we were on stage 24/7.

Our camp area became an unofficial activity center for children who came to us for stories and activities. Every day we had a Sunday school: we told flannel graph stories, sang songs and played games. Boxes of donated coloring books helped to keep the children busy.

Because of our experience providing children's entertainment in hospitals, and having had the first clown show in Taiwan, it was not long before we were called upon to perform. The children, especially, were in need of comfort and cheer. The military helped us to set up children's shows in several locations, and the response was overwhelming. Hundreds of traumatized children were now smiling, clapping and singing.

Soon we were working in cooperation with the Taiwan military to perform and offer aid in many different shelters, even traveling with the Red Cross up to the more remote mountain villages which had been devastated by the quake. Many volunteers from all over the island, from various backgrounds and religions came together to assist in the efforts, providing food and basic necessities for the thousands who were now homeless. Well-known singers and performers also offered to help in our mission of comfort and cheer.

There was hardly a moment to rest. When we finally sat down to rest at the end of a long day, a young soldier came up to us. His group was having some time off between shifts and wanted us to come spend time with them. We sang songs and told stories. They were eager to hear our message of comfort and hope in the midst of all this pain, and prayed together with us for God's love and care to watch over them.

They told us that in Taiwan all young men must complete two years of military service after they finish school. These soldiers were mostly between the ages of 18 and 22. These young men were at the forefront of the rescue operation and saw much destruction, suffering and death. I felt such high admiration for them. Even with their own homes destroyed and their families in crisis, these brave young men selflessly gave their all to rescue and care for others.

This country owes a great debt of gratitude to the rescue workers who risked their lives to save many others from the ruins, as large numbers of serious aftershocks threatened to bring down the already badly damaged buildings. Two days after the first quake, an aftershock measuring 6.8 brought down more buildings, trapping and killing rescue workers inside.

I must point out that throughout this time I was repeatedly impressed by the politeness and kind manners of the Taiwanese people, even under extremely difficult circumstances. I was surprised to see the calm and orderly fashion in which everyone operated. Whether moving to a designated safety zone or lining up for drinking water, not once did I see the "rush" or "panic" as is often depicted on television associated with such times of crisis. Instead, I saw people looking out for each other, knowing that each person's needs were as great as their own.

Shortly after the quake we made our way to a local convenience store which we heard was open. We needed batteries for flashlights and a few other essential items. We found the damaged store, broken windows and missing door, no electricity and no working cash register. People quietly rummaged through the piles of merchandise on the floor. On finding what they wanted, each person respectfully waited in a line to pay the store attendant standing outside on the sidewalk.

Driving through town I noticed department stores with windows and doors blown out, costly merchandise still filled the shelves or were scattered in piles on the floor. Yet looting was extremely rare. To take advantage of another's misfortune at a time like this would be an unthinkable crime.

Conditions were hard. I had to stand in line for hours to give my children a quick shower, or to have access to a sink to wash a few clothes. Rest was hard to come by. Privacy was nonexistent. The food was certainly not the best of Chinese cooking. It was often too spicy for the children to eat at all. Instead we fed them loaves of plain white bread which were distributed daily. Yet in spite of it all, we were healthy and well. The kids took it in stride and enjoyed the adventure that our outdoor camping environment afforded.

We carried a remarkable calm and strength, in spite of the hardships and the unnerving of constant aftershocks. Daniel's strength held up miraculously well. Needing to sleep upright due to his condition, he had been sleeping in the car for two weeks, while I stayed with our kids in the tent. Though not being able to be near him or care for him, I was not afraid for his safety. There was a profound feeling that there were forces at work here much larger than ourselves. God's hand of care had been so strongly evident around us that I could not doubt His ability to bring us through this safely. We were right where we were supposed to be.

Those few weeks following the earthquake were times of our greatest ministry. I felt grateful that God had chosen our little team, even with health problems, kids and all, and had placed us where we could be the greatest help to those around us. He helped us to forget our own troubles for a time, while we reached out to thousands around us whose needs were greater than our own.

While living through an experience such as this is a story all its own, one chapter to tell it is all I can spare. This book is not about Taiwan or earthquakes. It is about our family, and our fight against insurmountable odds to hold onto our faith and each other...

Chapter Three

Struggles in the Night

Leaving behind a country in crisis, we moved our family back to Houston to face a crisis of our own. Each night when I would go to sleep, I had to literally commit my husband's life into God's loving care. This was sometimes difficult to do. Whenever he fell asleep, the tumor would block his breathing passage. Attempts to breathe would be unsuccessful, so his body's involuntary reaction was to try harder, until his whole body would jerk hard and strain with the effort. Yet, still no air. 50 seconds, 60 seconds, 70 seconds. "Come on, breathe!" my aching heart would cry out. Finally, he would wake into a semi-conscious state and gasp loudly, getting only 2 or 3 breaths in. Then he'd fall back to sleep and start over.

He was only getting a fraction of the oxygen he needed. I remember one night when he was in the hospital hooked up to several machines with various alarm systems monitoring his vital signs. Every time he would start to drift into asleep all the alarms would go off, warning of suffocation or lack of oxygen. I finally had to ask the nurse to turn off the alarms and sit by to watch him instead, as the alarm was keeping him up all night. I said, "This is how he always sleeps, this is normal for him."

Each night Daniel strained harder in his sleep just to breathe than most people work in a day. It took a toll on his heart, and at times he would wake with severe heart pains, pounding heartbeat, and high pressure headaches, as his body tried to cope with the lack of oxygen. He would often dream that he was drowning, his physical struggle playing out in his subconscious mind.

At times I would sit awake for hours, praying and watching, then waking him if he couldn't breathe for too long. But eventually I had to trust him into God's hands, and go to sleep myself. I knew that Jesus would be there to watch over him all night.

Any kind of surgery to remove the tumor could be fatal, so the treatments were aimed at shrinking it a little at a time, just enough to keep it under control. Each treatment was excruciatingly painful, and the recovery was very difficult. For the first few days afterwards the tumor would swell even larger, and was in danger of suffocating him. For days Daniel would be unable to speak, eat or drink, and the pain was intense. His already critical breathing would become even more difficult. At times I did not know if he would live through the night.

Visitor from Beyond

It was on a night like this that something extraordinary happened. Daniel was struggling for any breath at all. I had sat by his side, praying for hours, till I finally fell asleep.

I awoke in the night to see a heavenly visitor in my room, standing right in front of me. I saw Colleen, our missionary friend who had died several months earlier. She was so beautiful. An aura of light radiated brightly all around her. Her long, red hair fell beautifully over her shoulders and down her back. My first reaction was one of peaceful amazement. She looked like an angel, glowing, soft, tender and caring.

Then a shocking thought hit me. "She's come to take Daniel to Heaven! It's time for him to go." I panicked!! I had heard stories before of the spirits of those who had passed on coming back to welcome and escort a loved one into the heavenly realm.

I ran into the next room and fell to the floor, crying out a desperate prayer. "Jesus, what's happening!?"

Then Jesus spoke to me. His voice was so clear, strong and reassuring.

"She came to watch over him so that you can sleep, and so he won't come Home before his time."

A wave of relief washed over me as I repeated these words over and over. Our heavenly visitor, though now hidden from my view, had been sent to watch over him. I had no need to stay awake fretting. He would not go Home before his time.

Facing Death –Embracing Heaven

At first I thought it was wrong to talk about death. I was afraid to broach the subject. We both knew it was a very real possibility, but I wanted to ignore it, to pretend it didn't exist. Yet as time went on, Daniel wanted to be able to express his wishes and make a few preparations in case he should have to leave us.

Daniel's peaceful and positive outlook slowly strengthened me and eased my fears. His requests were simple, but meaningful. He had certain songs that he wanted played at his funeral — songs of Heaven, life, and love. He did not want us to dress in black, the color of mourning. Instead he wanted his funeral to be a celebration of his life with us on earth, as well as his continued life in heaven.

We talked often about Heaven, what it would be like, and the wonders and joys we would share together there. Slowly, the vast gulf between this life and the next seemed to fade. Heaven became so real and close to me then, as though it were just another place we plan to go someday. And if Daniel should have to go on ahead of us, it would only be a temporary separation by circumstance. I would join him there again. The strange, dark fear of death was losing its sting. *"Where, O death, is your victory? Where, O grave, is your sting"* (I Corinthians 15:55).

Heaven! Such joy to know that there is such a place! What great peace there is in knowing that Jesus has assured us a place there with Him. No fear of death, no fear of what is to come, only joyful anticipation! It is a place where there is no more pain or fear. Sorrow and crying will flee away, and God shall wipe away every tear from our eyes.

Although we weep for the love that is lost to us, as for a friend that has gone away to a far country, *we do not grieve as those that have no hope* (1 Thessalonians 4:13). Death can never truly separate souls that are joined in Him. *"For God is Love"* (1 John 4:8), and this love, which He has created and given us for each other, will never die. He is the resurrection and the life. *"He who believeth on Me, will live, even though he dies"* (John 11:25).

Over time, I slowly broached the most difficult questions of all. What would I do if my husband died and I was left alone to raise our young children? At first it had seemed to me that life without Daniel would be the end my world, an unfathomable void, an unknown and scary future with no name and no face. I did not want to think about it or acknowledge the frightening possibility. But I eventually found that I had to face these fears if I was to have the strength to cope with the uncertainty of our future. I had to be able to picture life beyond the "what if". I had to learn to see life as continuing.

Although I had relatives in the U.S, there was no place that I really felt at home there. In fact, there was only one place that I truly did feel at home – Taiwan. I loved the people and the country. I also had friends and family there that I knew I could count on. And it was where the children had been so happy. I deeply missed our happy home there. I realize now that perhaps my desire to return to Taiwan, in a way, was also a subconscious need to run as far away as possible from these difficult memories, to return to a better and happier time.

I finally made up my mind. If the unthinkable happened and I had to pick up the broken pieces of my life and start over again, there was only one place for me to do that. I would take my children back to Taiwan. Although it was painful to even think of living life without Daniel, I felt some comfort in the thought that I would go back to the home I loved, and that I had friends and family there who would love and help me. This simple decision seemed to make it a little easier for me to bear. Perhaps only for the reason that putting a face on it had a way of making my future a little less scary, helping me to imagine and believe that life could go on.

I also found myself thinking about how I would support myself as a single mother, how I would raise my children without a father. I thought out each detail as best I could. Yet, in the end, so many questions could not be answered. I had to trust our lives and future into God's loving hands. I knew He would not fail me. Even as I passed through this *"valley of the shadow of death,"* I held onto the promise, *"I will fear no evil, for You are with me"* (Psalms 23:4). I held on to the promise that Jesus would not leave me alone.

He was becoming nearer and dearer to me than any friend. He was someone I could confide in and turn to for comfort and strength, as a woman does with her husband. Now, as I needed Him so greatly, I found Him to be more real and dependable than ever. This was the strength I held onto when my own human strength felt painfully weak and inadequate. The road before me at times seemed impossible and unimaginable. If I looked at the waves crashing around me, I could not bear it. I could only focus intently on my Master's face, or else, like Peter (Mathew 14:24-33), the waves would engulf me.

Fixing my eyes on Jesus (Hebrews 12:2) was the source of my strength. I had to learn to block out all else. I had to block out fear, and all the uncertainties in my life, and focus on the one thing I could be certain of – His Love. This I could stand on. If I truly believed that He loved us, then there was no place for fear.

The Will to Live

I sat by Daniel's hospital bed as he was recovering from one of his treatments. He was struggling to cope with the terrible pain, knowing it would be a long recovery, and he would have to repeat the whole treatment again after only a few weeks.

Being unable to talk at all, he slowly scratched on a note of paper, "I can't do this again. I would rather die..."

My heart wept for him. We both knew that to die painlessly in his sleep (suffocation was his greatest danger), and to be free from this body of pain and suffering seemed like a much easier road to take. But I held on tightly to the faith that we would overcome this, and have joy in our lives again.

When living becomes so much harder than dying, some people struggle with the will to live. They long for a way out, an end of their suffering. Daniel did not want to continue treatment, yet he kept going for me. Every time I sat beside him as he recovered from another painful treatment, I knew it was his love for me and for the children that kept him going.

Daniel wrote:

> *If it wasn't for my knowledge of our loving Savior and Friend, Jesus, and knowing that He was holding me through all of that, I don't know if I would have had the courage to go through with it. I found that when praying for faith, peace, etc, before going into surgery, I wanted to pray for courage. That was very important to have. It's almost like going into battle each time. Quoting Bible scriptures to myself was also a real help; it gave me the faith*

that all was going to be ok. I had to face these fears many times, and God's Word, prayer and praise were my only weapons.

Many times Daniel wanted to give up, to quit the treatments; the fight for life being so very hard. Instead he wished he could just walk away from it all and leave his life (or his death) in God's hands. Some people would call that faith. But there's a difference between faith and fatalism. Fatalism can be a way of just giving up. It takes more faith to go through the storm than it does to run away from it.

Don't get me wrong about faith!—There is a time when it is right to take a stand of faith, trusting only in God. Many people have taken such a stand and received wonderful miracles. That kind of faith comes from knowing with a certainty that such a stand is God's will for you. It is not passive faith. In our case I needed an answer from God for us to help me understand this subject of faith and fatalism. I felt a gentle nudge from God, and captured His voice in my heart again.

There is a time when you must fight for the life I have given you. I am pleased and would expect it of you. It is all a part of My plan, for as you cling to Me through this, many changes will take place—changes that could not otherwise be fulfilled. Sometimes it is necessary to fight for My will and grow stronger through it, rather than to yield to fate. That is not yieldedness, but pacifism.

For Daniel this was certainly true. The wonderful years we have shared together since then have been more than worth it all, and in the end, all that we gained from fighting through these difficult experiences more than compensated us. He is so glad now that he didn't give up, that he fought on till the dawn broke.

While preparing to write this chapter, I discussed this subject at length with my mother (herself a missionary for 40 years), who has suffered from fibromyalgia for the past 25 of those years.

She told me about a time following her successful treatment for breast cancer when the hardships she experienced through her physical weakness and pain made her feel so hopeless that depression had overtaken her, but she could think of no way to end her life without hurting her children, family and work. Although yearning for an end to her life and her struggles consumed her, her love for her children, and her commitments, constrained her.

Such depression is sometimes associated with severe stress, loss, life change, illness, disability, or among the chronically ill or terminally suffering. For some people, their suffering or troubles seem so bad, that they feel that death is the only way out.

At the time, when we are in the midst of the storm and the night seems so black with no way of escape, our vision is severely limited. But who can know what God will do a little while down the line, if we will just hold on a little longer.

My mother's life is a great joy to her now. She has had many outstanding and fulfilling experiences since then, has been a strength and a joy to her children and grandchildren, and has felt God's blessings in her life richly in recent years. Her full-of-faith, positive and peaceful attitude is a strength to all around her. She has seen her troubles become blessings in her life that have helped her in many ways.

How did she overcome her deep depression? First, she sought out the help and prayer of sincere Christian friends. This, she said, was the turning point for her, and greatly loosed the grip that depression had on her. Secondly, she held on!

Oh, how many victories are waiting for us if we just hold on a little longer. The sun will come breaking through the clouds. *"Your grief will be turned into joy..." (John 16:20).* *"Weeping may remain for the night, but rejoicing comes in the morning" (Psalms 30:5).*

Hold on to Hope

Even the black of the darkest night
Loses strength at the coming of dawn.
Eventually spring must be born anew,
Though the winter seems so hard and long.

In spite of the fury of the raging storm,
When its deafening winds rage against you,
Peace will come in the stillness again,
When sunlight breaks through to refresh you.

There's no sorrow too deep for God's love to reach.
There's no pain that His hand cannot heal.
Even the seeming impassable road,
Has a way through which He can reveal.

So hold on to hope, though the hope is so dim,
That its glow cannot even be seen.
The sun is not gone, it will soon rise again.
Things are never as bad as they seem.

Marie Morrow

Chapter Four

A TIME OF PEACE

After six months of treatment, Daniel's condition had improved considerably. He was breathing more easily and had recovered well. For the first time in many months he was able to lie down and sleep in a bed again. Previously, lying down, or even bending over would increase the blood flow to the tumor. This would cause it to swell instantly, adding to the pain and pressure and making him feel sick. For months he had slept in an arm chair or on the sofa.

We easily take for granted the simplest pleasures of life, like being able to lie down when we are tired, or stretch out our backs on a flat bed, or even bend over to pick up a piece of paper or tie a shoe. So, we counted our many blessings as we lay nestled in each other's arms and talked late into the nights. Life had slowed its pace, and the stress of the previous year was slowly melting away.

With this crisis now behind us, we decided to take a vacation and have some much needed time together to enjoy our family. Although we had traveled all over the world in our active missionary lives, we had not yet had the opportunity to explore the beauty of America.

We traveled for one month, first up to Colorado where the children experienced snow for the first time. Sledding was fun, though miserably cold. Driving through the Rocky Mountains was fabulous. We visited Daniel's sister and her family in Oregon, drove through the Sequoia National Park in California, saw the giant Sequoia trees, and spent the coldest night of our lives on the beautiful cliffs of the Grand Canyon.

This month of travel was a wonderful time of healing and renewal for us, as we visited friends and relatives, and soaked in God's beautiful creation.

On August 6th, 2000, God blessed us with another beautiful baby girl after only two hours of labor. During this short labor, I even surprised myself by managing, in the midst of the rush and heavy breathing, to wake my other three kids, get them dressed and brush their hair—between contractions—getting them ready to come with us to the hospital. Best of all, Daniel was able to deliver the baby. Everything was perfect.

Over the next few months we enjoyed a wonderful time of peace. With Daniel well and working again, we were able to get back to a more normal life. Those were fun days—home schooling my kids, cooking, cleaning, shopping, and being an all-around Super Mom, with my baby in one arm, stirring a pot of spaghetti with the other, and giving spelling tests to two separate grades at once. I loved it. This was the life I'd dreamed of since I was a child.

Looking Back

I had a fun and interesting childhood. My parents were missionaries and had moved with our family to Hong Kong when I was only three years old. We each began performing as soon as we were old enough to stand on a stage. Our family of little blonde kids, looked like we stepped right out of "The Sound of Music." We had the full Do, Re, Mi, Fa, So, La, and Ti. We immediately became very popular, performing everywhere we went. After all, it's not every day you see a troop of little American kids dancing and singing in Chinese.

When I was seven, my family left the city life and moved to a farm in a secluded ancient Chinese farming village that had never before let a foreigner in.—even the local government was unable to interact with them.

It was like going back in time a hundred years. The first year we used kerosene lanterns for light. In the second year we built a large generator that powered our house and our closest neighbors. By the third year we had run electrical wiring to the entire village and had plugged in to city power. Plumbing and water was another story. Every ditch had to be dug. Every pipe had to be laid. Septic tanks, city water, and a regular garbage disposal system gradually benefited not only us, but the entire village, as we put into action the commandment of Jesus to *"love your neighbor as yourself"* (Mathew 22:39).

It was a slow and patient life. At first our neighbors were cold and suspicious of the strange outsiders, resisting anything new, but in time they came to love and trust us. My parents became unofficial mediators and counselors, not only for physical needs, but also for prayer and comfort.

This sample of love in action eventually crossed the cultural boundaries and won their hearts. They saw, in an understandable, physical way what Jesus is all about. After all, Jesus was the first missionary. He came to live among us, as one of us, that we might better understand God's love for us.

I have many wonderful memories of growing up on this farm. Our little valley was surrounded by mountains on three sides, with a long beach only minutes from our house. I could hear the sound of the crashing waves from my bedroom window. Growing up with five brothers and a sister, there was no end of work and fun. We enjoyed hiking, swimming, horse-riding, milking cows and caring for the animals, as well as singing and ministering.

My best memories of all are of traveling through China— the mountains, farms, water buffalos, rickety rickshaws, roads crowded with bicycles, and mouthwatering 14-course Chinese banquets around huge round tables.

The Chinese holidays were always magical. The Lantern Festival was my favorite. In Cantonese tradition it is celebrated at the time of the Moon Festival in the fall. Try to imagine nighttime, softly lit with a large full moon, and thousands of people gathered on the beach and surrounding park areas, with beautifully colored paper lanterns of every style, shape and size. I would light a little candle and fix it in place in the center of my lantern, then unfold the paper lantern carefully up over it. Then I'd tie the string across the top of the lantern to a stick that I'd carry.

For my more adventurous brothers, there was the challenge of putting two lanterns on one stick. Then they'd tie the tops of two more lanterns to the tassels at the bottom of the first ones, and so on. The goal was to get eight or ten lanterns lit, balanced in perfect formation on one stick, and held up to admire before they all went up in flames. They would then kick sand over the fire and start again.

Chinese New Year is the biggest holiday of all. There are colorful dragon dances, lots of fireworks, and little red envelopes of money for the children. I enjoyed the Dragon Boat Festival with exciting boat races, and Moon Festival with lots of little moon cakes, as well as many other traditional events, holidays and parades. Chinese culture is rich and vibrant.

My love of the orient didn't stop there. When I grew up I found myself experiencing a whole different side of Asia, when I lived for several years in the great city of Tokyo, Japan. This was in sharp contrast to the relatively quiet and somewhat backward farm life I grew up with as a child. Tokyo is the most highly populated city in the world.

Japan is also a land of modern inventions. There is a gadget or gizmo for everything, from electronic toilet seats, to the automatic rice-measuring scooper. Even the simple fly swatter is not so simple. Every time I turned around there was something new and crazy to discover. Modern invention has found its way into every part of the Japanese home, but amazingly enough, they continue to preserve the unique and charming culture and traditions.

In Japan I worked at a Christian missionary school for several years. Children became my life. I loved the students and they loved me. It was both rewarding and fulfilling to see them grow and learn each day.

A Match Made in Heaven

The most wonderful thing that came into my life while living in Japan was my husband, Daniel. A handsome young American missionary, he was dedicated, funny, talented, romantic, caring, and great with kids. He was all that a woman could ever ask for! On top of all that, we could talk about everything, tell our secrets and share our dreams. We held the same passion for God and desire for a life in ministry work.

We were a match made in Heaven. But for some strange reason, I was the last person to find out. How we felt about each other seemed to be perfectly obvious to everyone else. My friends kept asking me when we were getting married, but I was in a state of denial. I thought about him all the time, couldn't wait for him to visit, and I clearly had the stars in my eyes, but I stuck to my answer: "There's nothing between us. We're just friends."

Of course, when he knelt on one knee and proposed to me on a perfectly romantic evening, I melted like butter and said, "YES!"

In fact, we loved each other so much that we got married three times. It's a little unconventional, I know, but there is a reasonable explanation. First, while in Japan we were married at the county office. It was a legal process that awarded us an official, and magnificently beautiful Japanese marriage certificate. Of course we still had the big formal wedding with our family and friends, complete with all the lace and frills, where we said our vows and were married once again.

Later, when in the United States, we needed to do some paperwork, but no one would acknowledge our Japanese marriage license. In spite of its ornate calligraphy and design, no one could read it. We soon found out it was cheaper and quicker to get married again than it was to get an official notarized translation. So, in a quaint little chapel, with only the kind reverend and his tape recorder playing the traditional wedding march, we said "I Do", and Daniel 'kissed the bride' one more time.

My husband had also been raised by missionary parents. Before living in Japan for seven years, he had lived mostly in countries of South America: Brazil, Argentina and Venezuela, and also in Mexico.

Not long after the birth of our first child, an opportunity arose for us, and we moved to Brazil. Daniel loved showing me all the places he enjoyed as a child. It is a beautiful country and we shared happy times in our ministry there. During our two years there we also had two more children.

Then eventually our little family made its way back to the Orient. My brothers in Taiwan had invited us to come and help with the ministry there. My background in Chinese made this transition fairly easy for me. Daniel, who had no trouble with Japanese, found the language to be quite challenging and I greatly admired his efforts. Chinese is a tonal language and exponentially more difficult.

We enjoyed Taiwan very much. After all, we had even had our honeymoon there years earlier. It is an island with beautiful contrasts: mountains, rivers, beaches, cities and farm land all fit perfectly together in 13,800 square miles. The culture is an amazing mixture of ancient Chinese tradition and cutting edge technology. The people are warm and friendly, and they quickly won our hearts.

I reminisced on these happy memories in distant places and dreamed of one day getting back to our work in Taiwan. Life had been so good to me, and I savored it even more now as we enjoyed the relative peace that we had found in this time of respite from illness. I enjoyed this opportunity to be the mom I wanted to be. I loved both the joys and the challenges of raising and teaching my kids. It was hard work but I really was happy at this stage of my life.

Little did we know that another storm was brewing just off the horizon...

Chapter Five

THE EYE OF THE STORM

I was trying to stay calm, but inwardly, I was panicking! Daniel's condition was worsening rapidly. The tumor had grown much more quickly than the doctors had anticipated. They had told us he would need treatment again in about four years. But now, after only one year it was already as bad as when we first started. He was back to sleeping on the couch, struggling for every breath. I spent many difficult nights camped out on the floor beside him.

Now, what had begun as a simple toothache had become a major crisis. Daniel had needed dental care for years but due to his high risk condition no dentist was willing to treat him. Since the tumor was also spreading deep into the gums surrounding his back teeth, we couldn't be sure what the problem was. The pain had become so unbearable, he was crying and shaking.

I was home alone with our four small kids, trying to figure out what to do for him. Every dentist and doctor we had tried had sent us away. His case was far too risky. Daniel's primary doctor, specializing in the treatment of his tumor, was out of town. Even Daniel's parents had gone for vacation to Florida. I didn't know where to turn for help. I felt so scared and helpless.

Then, bringing reinforcements of strength and comfort, some friends from our church answered my call for help. Just to have them by my side throughout this ordeal renewed my courage. Topaz took care of the kids, while her husband, Peter, drove us around to different specialists we were referred to, each one sending us on to another.

Daniel had several bad cavities and needed his wisdom tooth pulled. The simple dental work, under normal circumstances would be straight forward enough. However, Daniel's case was anything but normal. To make matters worse, strange and unexplained spots had shown up on repeated x-rays. The doctor said that the tumor may have spread into the bone.

These words came down on me like a giant boulder. I stepped out into the hall by myself for a moment. I didn't want Daniel to see me cry. My head was spinning. *What would this mean? How much worse would it get? What do we do now?*

We were told that before doing any dental work or other treatment, an MRI would be needed to see how far the tumor had spread and to assess the risks involved. Besides, nothing could be done without first consulting with his primary doctor.

By late in the day, we were finally able to get a message through to Daniel's doctor explaining the situation. His reply was very stern. "If you try to pull the tooth, YOU WILL DIE. There will be no way to stop the bleeding. Even a root canal will be life threatening. Don't do ANYTHING at all. Wait till I get back."

But that wouldn't be for two weeks, and he needed help now! So while everything within me was screaming to get help for him, we were told nothing could be done, and sent home with only some over-the-counter painkillers. Things looked pretty bad.

Friends from our church rallied to our aid, and before long a prayer chain had been put into effect. Friends and family across the country prayed for Daniel, and within a few hours he had fallen asleep – sweet relief for the moment.

But my mind was a whirlwind of emotion going a hundred miles an hour. The day had been so intense; I had hardly had time to breathe. I was struggling to find my place of inner peace, the kind that God can give even when the storm is raging all around. I had to get away from it all for a moment.

Curling up in my daughter's bunk bed, I found my little sanctuary. I realized then and there that I could not let this fear overcome me. I had been praying all day, but my desperate prayers were filled with fear reflecting my own untamed emotion. This kind of prayer is very weak, placing the focus on the problem, looking down at the waves around me. Real power in prayer comes from looking only at Jesus, asking in faith, and trusting in His love. This is where we find the calm in the eye of the storm, the place of stillness even in the midst of the billowing gale.

Once again, with tears in my eyes, I prayed for God to give me the grace to trust Him fully, and then I committed everything into His loving hands.

Oh, this is such a blessed peace! I felt it pour over me like warm sunshine, calming my troubled heart.

The heavenly voice spoke to me again saying:

"Carry this peace in your heart. Hold it close and don't give it up. You can have peace in the midst of the storm. It must be within. It comes from soaking up My presence. You will not be able to make it through the days ahead without that place of inner peace. But if you have it, nothing and no one can take it from you."

I was reminded of the song I loved to hear:

"You are the calm at the center of my storm.
When the cold wind blows,
You're the fire that keeps me warm.
When this cruel world lets me down,
I will rest inside your arms.
You are the calm at the center of my storm."

by Paul Overstreet

It is a never-ending miracle, how God can take a heart so sorely troubled, and breathe His soft breath of love upon it and transform it in His hand. He is so very near, so real, so dependable, and so comforting. I soon fell into a peaceful sleep.

Somehow, things didn't seem so bad after that. The storm of panic in my heart had passed, and I felt new courage to face the battles ahead. By the time Daniel's mom flew in from Florida the next morning, Daniel was already talking and even smiling again. I was amazed at this rapid change in his condition. Though the doctors couldn't do anything for him, prayer power had come to the rescue.

The following week, Daniel decided we needed to take some fun, quality time together as a family before he was to return to the hospital. He was feeling much better, and we wanted, for one day, to put all our problems aside and enjoy our time together.

Those are wonderful memories—a rich sweetness in the midst of our sorrow. We took a trip to Galveston, a beach resort area not for away. There we climbed the rocks and took pictures. Then we had a full adventure at a large castle park, as Daniel, pretending that the ground was lava, helped the children escape the great volcano by climbing throughout the whole park without touching the ground. He is just amazing with kids and has a way of bringing any game to life in such a dramatic way that they *live* the adventure of the experience with him.

In the evening we took a slow stroll through the large aquariums at Moody Gardens. It was a wonderful day.

I am so thankful that, over the years, and throughout our many difficulties, we took times such as these to enjoy each other. With so much stress in our lives, and our future so uncertain, these times renew our joy and make it worth it all. Now, as I look back over the years, I have many sweet memories mixed with the sad ones, and overall I feel richly blessed.

Money Matters

Shortly afterwards, Daniel and I were invited to attend a medical conference. These doctors were the best of the best, top experts in the field of treating vascular malformations. While there, Daniel was examined by a panel of doctors. If anything could be done, they would know.

They were experienced in using a new kind of laser surgery to treat this type of tumor. Although this treatment had been successful in many cases, because of the location and severity of Daniel's tumor, the treatment would be risky. And even then, it could only shrink the tumor little by little. It would still grow back again, possibly with other complications.

After further consultation with these doctors we were very surprised to find that, out of the many experts from across the country, the best in the world, there was only one doctor with sufficient experience to take on Daniel's difficult and unique case. He traveled around the world doing this type of surgery. He was clearly the leader in this field.

I remember feeling shocked at the discovery of what we were dealing with. Although this particular tumor is rare, it was the location and complications involved that really made for one of those exceptional few-in-the-world types of cases. All these other "experts" felt this case was beyond their expertise and thus were afraid of the liability of treating someone with such high risk factors.

We were relieved to find a doctor willing to help, but this also posed a problem for us: this doctor worked in Arkansas. In order for him to treat Daniel, we would have to move our family from Texas. A move of this kind was expensive and we needed a new vehicle before we would be able to travel. I had no way to get the money.

Daniel was now too weak to work. I was caring for him and our four young kids, as well as working part time to support us. We were already going into debt just to get by. I also knew that once Daniel started treatment, I would no longer be able to work to support us at all. He would need me at home with him all the time.

For months, we racked our brains for how to get the money we needed. I prayed and prayed, and tried everything we could think of. I wrote letters and appeals, but months passed and still nothing came. I was maxed to the bone with all I had to do already. What more could I try?

But God had many more lessons to teach me about faith and patience. I knew in my heart that God would not fail us. But when the answer delays long in coming, that's when our faith is tested.

It is impossible to describe what it's like – to feel that I was watching my husband dying in front of me and I was helpless to do anything about it, while help was waiting for him a few hundred miles away, but I just couldn't get him there. I had never worried much about money before, but now it seemed my husband's life would depend on it.

The Strength of a Friend

One morning I found myself feeling so desperate over the helplessness of our situation, I could not stop crying. I had tried to go through the motions, feed the kids, do the dishes, but the tears would not stop streaming. As Daniel slept and the children played quietly, I tried desperately to compose myself. I knew I had to be brave for the children's sake. I didn't want to let them see me cry.

For hours I tried to pull myself together, but nothing worked. I cried out to the Lord from the depths of my soul to please lift this burden of deep despair. I tried every tactic I knew to overcome this type of depression. I sang songs. I quoted Bible verses. I tried to read the Bible, but I couldn't even see the pages through my tears. I tried to praise the Lord for the blessings I did have; I tried to find a silver lining, but nothing could hold back the fountain of tears. How could I cry all day? My family needed me to be strong.

I had grown up with a strong foundation in God's Word. All my life His promises had always sustained me. Why, now, had the blanket of despair so fully engulfed me that I could find no relief?

Maybe I just needed to get out of the house. I packed up my baby on my back, my toddler in the stroller, and one more kid on each side of me, and headed to the park. I was glad there was no one there to see what a mess I was, and I thanked God that the kids were too busy playing to see what I was going through. But even the beautiful sunshine could not find its way through the dark storm clouds that surrounded me.

I knew I could not accept this despair. For my children's sake, for my husband's sake I had to find a way to rise above it. But I'd tried everything—or had I? I hadn't yet asked someone else to help me. The Bible says *"Two are better than one... if one falls down, his friend can help him up"* (Ecclesiastes 4:9, 10). This was something I could not overcome on my own.

So, I picked up my cell phone and called Topaz again, all the while still walking so the baby in the backpack would not cry. I told her of my desperate battle, and she prayed for me right there on the phone. She took up my cause, and pled for me in the courts of Heaven, as her husband, standing near her, joined in the fight.

Slowly, I felt my burdens lift and my tears dry. I felt the warm sunshine pour its rays deep into my heart. I found the victory I was searching for, the peace that Jesus offers us even in the midst of the severest of storms.

Why do we try to fight so long alone? Why do we fail to avail ourselves of the immense power available to us by asking others to pray for us? We are not meant to bear our burdens alone. His Word says to, *"Carry each other's burdens, and in this way you fulfill the law of Christ"* (Galatians 6:2). Oh, such strength is found in that bond of the spirit when two hearts unite and fight in prayer!

One difficult night, God again sent a visitor in the spirit to encourage us. But this time it was very different. In my sleep I dreamt of a Christian friend of ours who lived on the other side of the city. She was sitting by Daniel on the bed as he slept. Her hands were raised as she prayed fervently for him.

It was reassuring to see her faith as she fought for him before the Throne of Grace. When I woke, I had such a strange feeling about it. It seemed as if I could feel her presence. To my surprise, Daniel had also seen her in his dream as well. Could this just be a coincidence?

A few days later I spoke with this friend on the phone. I asked her about that night. She told me that on that same night she had woken up, unable to go back to sleep. She had a strong burden from the Lord to pray for Daniel, so she had gotten up and had prayed for him for several hours, and said that she felt quite near to us.

Amazingly, it was as though God had somehow bridged the distance between us in spirit through the vehicle of prayer. What an amazing God! What power we have through intercessory prayer!

Great Expectations

As the answers to our prayers seemed to be delayed, and were long in coming, our faith continued to be tested. Months passed, and we still had no money to get Daniel the medical care he needed. I reminded myself daily to look to God and not on the impossibility of our situation. I fought to stay positive and kept busy caring for my family. Each day brought with it new challenges, and through it I was learning to trust God anew each day.

I fell asleep one night heavily burdened for our great need. In a dream, I heard a song clearly playing, again and again. When I woke, the words of this song were still thundering through my head like the very voice of God.

I must have heard that song before somewhere. I didn't have any recollection of it, but subconsciously it must have been stored in some hidden corner of my memory. As I slept, God had brought it to life for me in full surround sound.

"Believe the unbelievable!

Receive the inconceivable!

See beyond our wildest imaginations;

Lord, we come with great expectations!"

The message was so clear. I woke up that morning with my faith renewed, my expectations full, and my heart rejoicing. I marveled at how God had, through one dream, so filled me with faith and anticipation that I was running over with joy.

A few days later I heard it on the radio: "Great Expectations," by Stephen Curtis Chapman. I got a copy of that song and listened to it a hundred times over. This song had been my special miracle. It represented a definite stand of faith—not a wishful hoping or longing, but a positive expectation of the full answer to our prayers.

Then all at once, by some magnificent miracle, the answers started pouring in—one donation, then another, and another. Within a two-week period, we had received all the money we needed for the van and the trip. We also received commitments for monthly financial support sufficient to cover our expenses for the duration of Daniel's treatments. It so touched my heart to receive letters and prayers from people around the world whom we'd never met before, but who had read our prayer request and had responded to our desperate need.

In addition to the financial assistance, we also received an invitation from a dear Christian family whom we had never met before, who lived near the city we needed to go to. They invited us to come and stay on their large, beautiful property. They had a mission center and would be able to take care of us and help with our children. God couldn't have planned it better.

They lovingly cared for us for the next ten months, giving us both the physical and spiritual support we needed. I was able to leave my children in their care, sometimes for days at a time, and be with Daniel when he went to the hospital for treatment.

I also enjoyed taking part in their active children's ministry and after-school program. At times, when Daniel was well enough, he was able to help out in various ways also. Our children made new friends and enjoyed the nature and open spaces our new location had to offer. Although we went through difficult times during our stay there, the Lord saw to our every need. The hand of His care was evident all around us, and with each new step our faith grew stronger.

...But would our faith be strong enough to get us through what was coming next?

Chapter Six

LIFE CAN CHANGE IN AN INSTANT

"Of course it won't be cancer." I said confidently to a friend. "After all we've been through already, what are the chances?! Don't worry. The tests are only a formality."

Other than the difficulties associated with my pregnancies, or the tiredness of being a busy mom, I had always enjoyed excellent health. So when I went in for surgery to have a tumor removed from my uterus, I never doubted that it would be anything other than a routine surgery with a speedy recovery.

I had endured two months of hardly being able to keep any food down, losing a lot of weight, struggling with weakness, tiredness, etc. The severe sickness I was experiencing was due to abnormal hormone levels, caused by the rapidly growing tumor with which I was "pregnant". Surgery would bring relief of all these symptoms and I'd be back on the road to a normal life.

Little did I realize how much my life would change from that point on. While I would eventually recover from cancer, my body would never be the same again. The days of being a strong and healthy super-mom would be only a memory of my past.

After my initial surgery to remove the tumor, weekly blood test were needed to monitor these hormone levels. If all is well the hormones would continue to fall, and eventually return to zero. If the tumor is malignant however, the hormones would rise again as the tumor grows back or spreads further.

I could not even consider the possibility of cancer. After so long fighting for my husband's health; I was confident nothing else could go wrong. After all, I was supposed to be the strong healthy one. So while I continued having my weekly blood tests, we began preparations for our move back to Texas. I thought at that time that this was faith, but perhaps it was just denial.

We had left our home in Houston for the sake of Daniel's medical needs. His condition had improved and we were feeling quite hopeful about the future, believing that the worst was now behind us. Since Daniel was no longer receiving treatment, we were ready to go back to Houston. I was also recovering well; though still somewhat weak from the surgery, the more difficult stage of sickness had passed. I was happy to be busy organizing, packing and planning. Everything was going along as scheduled.

It was late afternoon, and I was just finishing up a little last minute packing and saying goodbye to friends. We would be leaving first thing the next morning. Then the phone rang. I listened in shock as the doctor gave me the results from my latest blood test. The hormone levels had risen drastically, indicating that the tumor had returned, as well as confirming that it was indeed malignant. He wanted me in for another surgery by seven o'clock the next morning. I had cancer!

Somehow, when you hear those words, the world seems to stop. *This is not possible. There must be some mistake. This can't be happening to me. What about our plans?* I sat stupefied on the end of my bed.

Daniel was out with the kids picking up supplies for our trip. Only moments before, I had been working in high gear to have everything ready before he got back. We were hopeful and excited. Everything was looking up. Now, suddenly, with one phone call, our lives would change in an instant. I was numb with shock.

I felt a dizzying array of questions, a confusing muddle of thoughts. I desperately needed someone to be there to pray with me right then. In answer to my prayers, I saw a car coming up the driveway. It was a good friend, James, from the local mission center. I told him what I had just learned, and together we committed all of it to the Lord. It was such a strength to me just to have someone there to lean on and to pray with.

As I went into surgery the next morning, I had total peace in my heart about everything. We were in God's hands. All we could do—needed to do—was trust.

In the Oncology Ward

It was not until I walked into the oncology ward of the hospital following my second surgery that the reality of the whole cancer thing really hit me. I sat in the waiting room taking the whole scene in. Along one wall was a display of wigs and hats for sale. Daniel and I looked at them for a while, but didn't say much.

Sitting across from me was a young woman about my age. Her head was bald. Her face was pale and sickly. Her tiny frame was little more than bones, and she had a tube coming out of a hole in her chest. Looking at her I couldn't help but wonder what the future held for me.

Many thoughts went through my mind, thoughts that could not be put into words. I had come to hospitals many times to comfort and encourage other patients. Now, I was the patient. I felt so strange and disoriented.

My oncologist seemed cold and hard, talking about my case as if it were all facts, statistics and procedures. Maybe this was the result of working with pain and death for so long. I felt intimidated and uncomfortable talking with him. Or was it just the subject matter that was so difficult? It was his job to tell me the facts, and sometimes there's no easy way to say it.

He made it clear to us that the cancer had become aggressive. The pathology results from my last surgery showed the cancer had progressed to the next level, and had invaded my uterus.

I spent all day doing x-rays, CAT scans, MRIs, blood tests, and every other test imaginable. The doctor's first concern was to see if the cancer had spread to any other organs. The initial results of which were encouraging. But cancer cells traveling in the blood could show up anywhere. This type of cancer most commonly spreads to the lungs and brain where it is much harder to fight, so a quick and aggressive approach was important.

The doctor was stern. He said I needed a total hysterectomy: the removal of my uterus, cervix and ovaries. Following this, I would need several months of chemotherapy. With a swift and aggressive approach, there was a high chance of beating this cancer. But he warned that the cancer can spread rapidly to more delicate organs, greatly reducing chances of successful treatment.

After we came home that day, I sat in the car in the driveway for several hours. I wasn't ready to face anybody.

My head was spinning in a whirl of confusion, like sitting in a fog so thick I could hardly breathe.

I prayed desperately, but could find no clear direction. It seemed like God wasn't answering me. Now I understand that I just needed more time to get over the shock and panic in my heart. I needed to find my center of balance, so to speak, that place of quietness within my heart.

It's hard to hear the still small voice of God when your emotions are thundering like a waterfall. I really tried to quiet my spirit, but it was not something I could do myself. I needed time to recover from the stress of the day, time to clear my mind, time to rest. It took several days before I was ready to face this again.

Hands of Love

The hysterectomy was the hardest thing for me to face, something I did not even want to consider at first. As impossible as it seemed, I still held onto a flicker of hope deep in my subconscious that someday we could get past all these difficulties, and still have the life of our dreams. I hoped that when the time was right God would see fit to heal Daniel and give us back the life we wanted. Since the time we got married we had often talked about having a big family. I had dreamed of it all my life, so was delighted to find that my husband-to-be shared my feelings. I had always thought seven children seemed to be the perfect number for a big happy family.

So now to have this surgery at only 26 years of age, would seem to cut out a part of my life which I would never be able to get back again. It meant closing the door on a chapter of my life which was very special to me.

There is something magical about being pregnant, the feeling of the baby kicking and moving inside of me. I loved delivering that baby into the world. I loved holding and nursing each one and watching them grow, talk and walk. Then there is the joy of sharing your lives together, teaching them and being friends with them. For me, childbearing has been a thrilling and vastly rewarding experience. Every child is a unique and special gift from God, a wonderful miracle of His creation.

We researched many stories of women who have had this surgery. Though most said it takes eight months to a year to fully recover physically, some women claimed that the emotional scars last forever. They feel as though a part of their womanhood is taken from them, leaving an emptiness in their lives. I feared that this would happen to me. I was afraid that if I went through with this surgery, I'd never be able to see a baby again without crying.

Jesus soon comforted my heart about the surgery and told me that I would never look back with remorse on this decision. He fulfilled His promise wonderfully, giving me total and unwavering peace about it. Somehow He reached deep into my heart and re-wired my thoughts and feelings, changing the way I felt forever, so that I never did have any feelings of loss in this area of my life

We did everything we could to prepare physically, mentally and spiritually for the upcoming surgery. I would be having a total abdominal hysterectomy. We found some very helpful web sites that gave us a better idea of what to expect, the best of which was hystersisters. com, a support site for women recovering from this type of surgery.

It's strange how little things had such a big effect on me. I had so far been pretty brave, trying hard to stay positive about it all. Then the doctor told me that in my case since a more extensive surgery was required for the cancer, a vertical incision would be needed instead of horizontal. A hidden panty-line scar I could live with, but now I would end up with a big, ugly scar from my naval down to my pelvic bone. I know this sounds like a silly thing in the midst of all the rest, but for me it was the last straw.

The stress and emotion of it all caught up with me, and I cried hard. I'd had four kids without a single stretch mark on my belly. I kept a nice figure, slim and in good shape. Now I feared that this huge, frightening scar would stand as a permanent reminder of this terrible ordeal. I was losing a part of my femininity, even if no one thought so but me.

My husband then did the sweetest thing possible. He somehow understood my deep need to feel better about myself, to know that he loved me and thought I was beautiful, no matter what. The day before surgery he took me out for a photo shoot. He is an excellent photographer, and on that day I was his work of art. He projected such compassion and tenderness in his hands as he combed my hair just right, adjusted my clothing and made sure the lighting was perfect. He took me from one location to another to get the different background scenery, and doted over me as an artist over his masterpiece.

I felt so loved and appreciated. Instead of fearing and dreading the surgery ahead, we spent the day just enjoying each other. It was the best gift he could have given me. I felt calm and peaceful. It is a memory I will always treasure.

The Voice on the Phone

I had read and studied all I could, and I thought I knew what to expect: "the worse pain possible and a long hard recovery." But let me tell you, nothing could have prepared me for what I experienced. I'd had a number of surgeries before, but nothing like this. It was worse than any pain I had imagined. Even the morphine I was given seemed only to take the edge off for a few minutes.

Once I woke up from surgery, the whole world around me seemed to stop. Minutes went by like hours. The long days and nights all blurred together. I had brought books to read and music to listen to during my recovery time, all left untouched in my bag. Even soft music or television was more than I could handle.

Yet as difficult as it was for me, I knew this was the hardest thing for Daniel to go through. He had faced the anxiety of waiting through my three and a half hour surgery, before hearing any news of my condition. Afterwards he said, he felt as if a part of his heart was being ripped out from him, when he had to watch me suffer so severely. I found out later that each day when he came to be with me, he would sit in the parking lot and cry for 30 minutes before he could even come in. Like a true hero, he stood strong by my side, always positive and encouraging. He wouldn't let me know until much later how hard he was taking it.

The most difficult part of the recovery was two times each day when nurses would make me get up and walk in the halls. My pain was already maxed out. I needed help just to change positions in the bed. I couldn't even sit up unaided. How on earth was I supposed to get up and walk? But the doctors insisted that walking was a necessary part of the recovery. Somehow each day, leaning heavily on my husband's arm, God gave me the grace to take each impossible step.

My doctor said that after the hysterectomy I would need four or five days of recovery in the hospital and then two weeks of recovery at home. What this really means is that the insurance company will only cover five days of hospital care, and after two weeks the main danger of infection and complications is passed, so the doctor's job is over. If you have the same surgery in England you are required two weeks hospital stay and six weeks of nursing care.

My fifth day was the worst yet. The pain was unbearable. It was the most intense pain of my life. *Could this really be normal, or is something terribly wrong?* I could not hold back the tears as I begged my husband to call friends from our church to pray for me. At the same time my doctor came in to check on me. He said that I have recovered well and I'm ready to go home. He signed the release papers and told the nurse to get me ready to go.

They have got to be kidding. How can I survive the trip home in this condition? I could not bear to even move, much less to be moved. I told the nurse my objection.

She replied that there was nothing further they could do for me, and that the pain would be the same here or there. Maybe so, but I was in no condition to travel. I was shocked at how insensitive and uncaring she was. I was just a patient with a chart, and the chart said 'discharged'.

It was a great comfort to know that my friends and family were praying for me. I could hardly focus on a prayer myself, and I could not hear the sweet voice of comfort from Jesus that I so longed for, but my friends were interceding for me.

Then, when I needed it most, a friend called the hospital room and said that, while praying, she had received a message from Jesus for me. My husband held the phone to my ear as she read it to me. Each word she read brought a wave of comfort and relief. Tears streamed down my face as I listened. A warm presence enveloped me, and I could feel Jesus so near, as if I could hear His voice whispering the words Himself into my ear over the phone.

This was the miracle I so desperately needed. His healing touch washed over me. The pain was easier to bear. My spirit was calm and my courage renewed. I thank God for the grace He gives even in the fiercest of storms. I can't imagine going through those things without Him by my side.

A few hours later I was sent home. The nurse who wheeled me down to the entrance was very rough and careless, hurting me badly, but I could hardly even speak, and was unable to raise my voice to protest. Yet still feeling the strength of God's presence with me, I held onto Him and His grace to endure. I was thankful to be going home.

During this time, our children held up remarkably well. While I was recovering, Daniel was still not fully well and was daily struggling with his health and strength. I am very grateful to our faithful friends at the mission center who came each day to pick up the children and helped care for them when I was ill. I also couldn't have done it without my dear sister, who came to live with us for a time to care for me during my recovery period and gave my children the attention I couldn't.

The children showed amazing maturity for their young age, learning to look out for each other and be responsible. Of course, the stress that they were going through at seeing first their father and then their mother so sick, showed up at times. Besides our one-year-old baby still in diapers, the older kids—aged five, six, and seven—began wetting their beds regularly, a sign of emotional stress. But besides this they seemed to take it all in stride. It was a comfort to my heart, as a mother, to see the peace that the children had throughout this time, in spite of some setbacks. They seemed quite happy and would play peacefully together for hours.

We always made an effort, whenever we were well enough, to go out with the children, or do special activities with them at home. Our times together have been fun and meaningful. The hardships we have been through have brought us closer together as a family, and have helped us to value our relationships all the more.

Chapter Seven

DOUBLE TROUBLE

It was a day to remember. Daniel and I were both seeing doctors—in two different hospitals, in two different cities—at the same time.

Daniel had been sent to see a specialist in a city six hours away. A painful new and unusual development in his tumor had doctors fearing the possibility of a malignant growth. He was away for several days. There he had tests and a biopsy done. It was a risky procedure, causing excessive bleeding from the tumor. This was a scary and somewhat traumatic experience for him. I felt so bad that I could not be there with him when he needed me.

Meanwhile, at the oncology center, I was being told by my doctor that my latest blood test showed high levels of hormones, indicating that the cancer was still prevalent. I would need to start chemotherapy right away. It was a difficult day for me at the hospital, as I did tests, tests and more tests and was briefed all about the chemo procedure and side effects. I missed the strength and comfort of having Daniel beside me.

The following week was a tense time of waiting as we held our breath for the results of Daniel's biopsy. I could not imagine both of us having cancer at the same time. After all, how much worse could things get? That was a subject so big in itself that neither of us dared to talk about it. Instead, we focused our minds on the Lord's promises. I sought His answers to my questions, and He filled me with His peace and gave me a message of hope and commendation.

"Your faith is so simple. Oh, how I love such faith. I measure each ounce of your pain with the most careful hand. I am with you through this, as with every other test. You have made it this far, and you will make it again. Fear not. This has not come to stay. It is but for a moment, and you will go on to receive the promises I have given to you. You are my prized warriors of the faith, and I love to show you off. To do that, I put you up against many a worthy adversary, that you may prove yourself again that they cannot defeat your faith."

What a wonderful commendation. It doesn't seem fitting for Him to commend us for our faith when He is the one who gives it to us in the first place. Time and time again He renews our courage, fills us with supernatural peace, and gives us the faith to trust Him in the most difficult circumstances. He's the one who should get all the glory, yet He commends us.

These are beautiful manifestations of His love to us, even as unworthy as we are. We simply make the decision to trust Him, and then He gives us the peace and grace to do it. It's a matter of yielding—a conscious decision to run to Him and give Him all our problems, then He does the rest.

The chemo was a major fear for me to face. I had already been so weak and sick, on one occasion even being taken to the hospital in an ambulance. How would I handle the terrible side effects—severe nausea, vomiting, weakness and many others?

I was also afraid of losing my long blond hair which flowed to my waist and my husband was so fond of. I had thought that it would gradually thin out and maybe I wouldn't really lose it all, so I was shocked when the doctor said I would lose *all* my hair within the first few days of treatment.

I actually took this the hardest. The sickness I felt I could be brave enough to bear, but there is something about losing all my hair to chemo that seemed like a bad nightmare. It is the picture of the cancer sufferer so embedded in my mind from the tragic movies I had seen, and of the cancer patients we had visited in hospitals in the course of our missionary work. I cannot explain why this was so hard for me. I was not particularly proud about my hair, but the thought of losing it in this way scared me greatly.

Before beginning chemo my husband helped me shop around for a wig. I also tried out pretty hats and scarves, a few of which I felt were quite becoming. It is a very somber feeling, shopping for wigs. Daniel was so kind, always assuring me that I would be beautiful no matter what. He even did some research, to see if my long hair could be cut and made into a wig of my own. Although that service is not available here, I was touched that he tried.

One day I had a beautiful conversation with Jesus that put my mind at ease and helped to calm my fears. These notes are taken from my journal.

My mind is racing in a whirlwind of questions. Then slowly a gentle peace sets in and I hear the familiar voice I love.

"Can you feel My presence so close, so real to you at this moment?"

Yes, I could feel Him so tangible, surrounding me like a warm breeze. I sat for a long moment soaking in His peace.

"This is My loving hand over you at this moment, all around you, enveloping you, and holding you. Can you feel any doubt, any fear, when I hold you like this?"

No, none at all. I felt perfect calm in my mind as His peace replaced my fear.

"I am just as close and real as I was with Daniel in the lion's den (Daniel 6:16-23), or with My children in the fire" (Daniel 3:17-23).

"Please know that I would never allow this if it was not for your good, and if I would not give you every bit of the strength you need to go through the fire. My grace will be sufficient, and you will come to know Me in a new way. This is a great humbling for you, but don't be afraid of it. It is part of the experience that

will change you forever, and make you fit to do My will. You have sought My higher calling, and have found it on the path of humility."

I could see how this brief time of suffering was giving me valuable insights into the world of those suffering from cancer. I could see their needs, feel their fears and heartaches. I knew that someday God would use this for good in my life, and enable me to reach out to comfort other cancer suffers, in a way that I would not have been able to do before.

I mustered up my courage, and turned my focus and attention to preparing mentally, physically and spiritually for the difficult road ahead. I researched all I could about chemotherapy and braced myself for the worst.

A Day of Miracles

Then everything turned around so suddenly! Only two days before I was scheduled to begin chemo I received a call from my doctor. My latest blood test results came back so low that even my skeptical doctor had to admit he was surprised, and said to hold off on the chemo. It had been a miracle!

That same day we received another phone call with the results from Daniel's biopsy—no cancer! It had been an abscess within the tumor, which by this time was already healing quickly!

Daniel and I went out to a restaurant together to celebrate. It was the first time in a month that I had been out of the house anywhere besides the hospital. Significantly, that night at the restaurant Daniel was able to eat solid food for the first time in two months, after living on only blended drinks and soups. It was as if the storm clouds had parted and we were seeing the long awaited sunshine again. Our hearts were overflowing with praise and gratitude!

While I never did have to go through with the Chemo, I was thankful for all that I learned during this time that I had studied and prepared for it. I had faced a variety of emotions and fears, and as I did, I found myself filled with compassion and deeper understanding for all those who walk this hard road. In this I could see the fulfillment of the words Jesus had told me, and I rejoiced in His unfailing love.

For the next few months I continued my weekly blood tests to monitor my hormone levels as they slowly went back to normal. My doctor frequently reminded me that the cancer could still show up again.

Then one day I received the results of my latest test. This time the news was *not* good. The doctor wanted to see me immediately, and recommended I begin chemotherapy, starting on Monday. He said, "You dodged the bullet before, but this time I don't think you can get out of it."

I could hardly believe this was happening again. Could it possibly be that after doing such an obvious miracle for me the last time, I was now supposed to go through with the chemo? Or was this the time to take a stand of faith and hold God to His promises?

As I sat in the examination room waiting for the doctor, my thoughts were directed to Heaven. I knew I needed to give the doctor an answer, as he was anxious to schedule my chemo. But first, I needed to get my answer from God.

The answer I received was short and to the point. *"Do not call anything impure that God has made clean"* (Acts 10). The meaning was clear to me: God had already done the miracle before, and there was no reason to doubt that miracle now. I firmly believed that if God had said it, then it was so. There was nothing further to worry about. But I did not want to get into an argument with my doctor about it: faith was not something he could easily understand. Instead, I insisted that he repeat my blood test before making any further plans.

The next day my test results came back fine. We had withstood another test, and had the rare blessing of being able to rejoice in our miracle a second time. Through each new experience we were learning to trust in God, increasing our faith for the bigger miracles yet to come.

The Value of a Promise

How much is a promise worth? Is it worth any more than the paper it is written on? What is a promise anyways? Is it the act of a signature, a handshake or pinky promise?

Primarily the worth of a promise lies in the trustworthiness and reliability of the one making it. It depends also on the ability of the promise maker to fulfill their word, if it is realistically within their power to do what is stated. We also look at the person's history and see if he has proven himself in the past. There is also the factor of the unpredictable which can change the circumstances surrounding the promise. If I promise to take my child to the zoo this weekend, but a storm blows in that day, my promise is void by default.

This is the question of the ages that has been asked all through the generations. Can God's promises really be counted on? Are they merely beautiful, poetic words intended to soothe us with a pleasant sound? What do they mean to me personally?

Firstly I look to the reliability of the promise maker, God. He is God. He is able. Whatever He promises, He is able also to perform. Next I look to past experience. Again and again I have put His promises to the test and found them to be sure and dependable. I have cashed the checks of scripture and have found them to be payable on demand each time. I have followed His personal words of guidance to me and He has never failed to lead me right.

Most importantly, I have learned also to trust in His promises regardless of circumstances because my faith is not in the specifics of the promise itself, but in the promise maker. I don't have to understand exactly how or when He will fulfill that promise, I trust Him to do what is best because He loves me. He has never failed me before, why should He begin now? *"Not one of all the good promises the LORD your God gave you has failed. Every promise has been fulfilled; not one has failed. (Joshua 23:14)"*

This is the premise of faith on which I was standing as I looked with joy and anticipation at the new promise that had been placed in front of me. God had spoken as clearly as ever, several times to be sure. He had given us a promise for Daniel's healing, that this tumor would no longer have the power over him. Although we did not yet know how or when this promise would be fulfilled, we had heard a definite message, telling us that God's hand had moved on our behalf to do something wonderful. We did not see an obvious change at first, yet a miracle had indeed come. Daniel had been inoculated with a portion of healing that would be sufficient to sustain him.

Our overall outlook on how we viewed Daniel's tumor changed radically from that point on. No longer was it a thing to be feared. I mediated on the scripture, *"This sickness will not end in death. No, it is for God's glory so that God's Son may be glorified through it"* (John 11:14).

The heaviness of his affliction still weighed on him. The pain and fatigue was something he still had to cope with. The physical circumstances hadn't changed. From the medical viewpoint, this was something that Daniel would have to deal with for the rest of his life, and they could not say how long it could be kept under control. There was little that could be done medically; even the best laser treatments work from the surface and cannot reach deep into the tumor where the real growth is. Each treatment also carries great risk. We still had every reason to fear.

Yet, in the spirit, everything had changed. Our attitudes and our conversation reflected this change. We now believed *God's* Word over the doctor's word. Somehow, everything seemed easier after that. In spite of occasional battles with discouragement, doubts or fears, we stood on the promises, and found them to be strong and stable indeed.

Part of this miracle came in the form of a new C-PAP machine he started using to aid his breathing when he sleeps.

The $1500 machine had been donated by the manufacturer brand new. The machine blows air through a tube to a mask strapped onto his face. The air pressure is electronically controlled and monitored to force the air through, keeping his breathing passage open. This enabled him to sleep well for the first time in years.

But sleep was only part of the answer. Relief of painful pressure and sickness, being able to eat solid foods again and overall strength, were among the miracles which gradually became more evident, allowing him to get back to a reasonably normal life, and to have energy to live, work, and play with the children again. Contrary to medical reasoning, without any further dangerous and painful treatments Daniel's condition dramatically improved. As a result his overall health and quality of life were greatly impacted for the better.

Now, as I look back over the years since then, I marvel at how the Lord has kept Daniel safely through all the storms that came our way. Though his tumor has continued to grow and spread further up into his head, he has been sustained by a touch of healing that keeps him going on in spite of it. Although he has not been physically healed, he is a walking miracle! This, in a way, is even more amazing to me. I remember how seriously we fought for his life for so long, the severe warnings from doctors of his delicate condition, the rapid growth of the tumor that was choking out his very breath. Yet to see him now, still going strong, without medical intervention, in spite of the continuing unstoppable growth, this is truly a miracle.

If you met him today, you would never know that there is anything wrong with him. He carries his cross bravely and with grace. He has his limitations which certainly impact his daily life. He cannot lie down even for a few minutes, cannot sleep without his machine and must keep his head upright. But by God's grace Daniel has been able to carry on and live a productive, happy and normal life in spite of it, pursuing his dreams and sharing in the joys of our family. I have never feared again for his life.

Our trip back to Houston was a happy one. It was the closing of a difficult chapter of our lives, and we looked ahead with hopeful anticipation. Things were looking up. I was also recovering, slowly but surely. Though still very weak, I had no further signs of cancer. Our mission here had been accomplished. We were eager to leave.

After the first day of travel, we pulled into a beautiful state park that had accommodations for the night. We arrived early with several hours of daylight left for the children to play and explore. That evening our fluffy, orange and white cat gave birth to five adorable kittens. They were born right there with the children excitedly watching.

It was a special day for us, as we celebrated a time of new life and new beginnings. As the sun went down, we roasted marshmallows over the fire, and marveled at all that God had done for us.

Chapter Eight

LEARNING TO SMILE AGAIN

Tests showed nothing wrong, but I was not well at all. During the next two years following my fight with cancer I still did not fully recover. I couldn't understand why. I was often exhausted and in pain. My whole body would ache like the flu, coupled with more severe localized pains at times. My mind would get so muddled; I couldn't focus or think straight. I could get lost in my own neighborhood, only blocks from my house. I was confused and forgetful. Although I worked hard trying to get back to a normal life, I had to rest often, and was constantly faced with my limitations.

I simply wasn't the strong woman that I used to be, and it was very hard for me to except that. I had high expectations for myself of what I thought a mother should be and do. I carried a lot of guilt and worry about the things that I couldn't get done. I had to let go of striving for the standard of perfection I held for myself, which I felt was so right and necessary, and learn to enjoy the life that I had.

I had to learn how to have fun again, an important part of healing and recovery. The previous years had been very difficult and stressful for all of us. We needed time to heal, physically, emotionally and spiritually. We needed to get connected, enjoy each other, and be happy in the Lord. Sweet Jesus spoke to me repeatedly about this, reminding me to slow down, relax, and be happy. His Words were always comforting, helping me to see things from His heavenly perspective.

"Stop trying so hard, and relax. Take it easy and have fun. That is what I expect of you. I give you one goal for each day. Do something fun! You're coming out of a very difficult time, and part of the healing process is to laugh. Be happy and content in My love. I want to see you smile.

"Remember, this time was equally difficult for the kids. They haven't seen your sweet and happy self for a while. They miss you. You're trying too hard, trying so hard to please Me that you forget that I'm trying to please you."

"Quit trying to perform or live up to holiness. You will understand a big part of My nature when you learn to have fun and experience My joy. Lighten up, on yourself and on others, all the way around. Make an effort to experience My joy to the full, and to feel the freedom of the spirit, to learn the happy side of Me. For you have done well in other aspects, and have tried hard to please. But until you learn My joy, you will miss out on what I am truly all about."

"Daniel has had it pretty bad this last year, much more than you know, and it's still a very sore spot for him. He loves you so and feels your pain. Please help him recover. This heavy-

heartedness will wear him down. Be happy, for his sake. Let him see the happy girl he married. Don't let the weights of life steal your joy and your beauty. Shine on for Me. I can and will do it through you. Refuse to talk about problems, for his sake. Refuse to be discouraged, or murmur, or talk about things you can't do."

"Be happy! Rejoice! Now is the time to praise. Let your whole spirit and countenance praise Me. I love to see you excited and having fun! Be happy. Rejoice in your salvation, rejoice in your healing. You've been through a lot and have come out smiling. Don't let the world steal that smile."

Isn't it special how God *wants* to see us smile? He wants to see us happy just like a father likes to see his kids happy. How contrary to the picture many people have of God, as a strict task master waiting to judge us for our mistakes.

There is a lot of stress in our lives at times, but God is smiling kindly at us saying, *"The joy of the Lord is your strength"* (Nehemiah 8:10).

Being so very weak forced me to slow down and reevaluate my priorities. I simply couldn't do all that I used to do, or all that needed to be done. My strength was so limited I had to ask myself, *what use of my time is going to make the biggest difference? If I only have a few minutes to work, what should I do with it?* The more I thought and prayed about it, the more I realized that nothing was more important than the people in my life. When my children grow up, will they even remember if I folded the laundry or had everything organized? Maybe not, but they would be more likely to remember the times when I listened to them, or read stories together.

Whenever my focus was on accomplishments and goals, I would always end up frustrated, tired and in pain. I was impatient to get back to "normal" — the strong, healthy person that I used to be. I wanted to keep a daily schedule, teach the kids, clean the house, cook the meals and be involved in ministry again. Instead, I was learning patience and love. God did not want me to go back to being the old me. He was making me into a new person in Christ Jesus. I was learning a whole new set of priorities.

I realized that I had to change my focus, learn to get my eyes off the problems. I would stress all day about my messy house to where that was all that I could see. I was missing out on my children's lives! I had to constantly remind myself to let my hair down, relax and enjoy my family. When we focus only on work, our lives can feel dry and meaningless, but if we make time for love, we come to life like flowers in the spring.

I began to check myself regularly. "When I look around my house, do I see work or people, burdens or blessings? When my children speak to me, am I really listening, or am I thinking about the dinner? Relationships are built moment by moment, day by day, year by year. What can I do today to build up my family? How can I show my love to them in a way that they can relate to?"

The next big question was, "Where do I get time for this, when I can't even put away the laundry?" Jesus showed me to look for the moment fillers, the small minutes of time throughout the day when I could show love. This was a breakthrough for me. I realized it didn't have to be a big family outing or a two-hour scrabble game. It had to be simple.

When my toddler was fussy, I could take her on my lap for five minutes and read her a story. When my son asked a difficult question, instead of brushing him off, I could take a few minutes to look it up on the internet together. I could take a little more time for a hug and a kiss when the kids were grumpy. I could smile more at the kids. This is important. A smile says, "I love you, I'm happy being with you, and everything is O.K."

It's amazing what a little love can do. We think we are too busy, but it's not a matter of time, it's a matter of priorities. Going through severe illness often makes people re-examine their lives and priorities. But why wait until you are sick or dying to start taking stock of your life? Why not think about it today, while you are still alive and strong enough to do something about it? If you knew you only had a little time left, would you stress about the laundry or the garbage? If this was your last week to be with your family, would you spend it preparing for a board meeting? How do you want to be remembered?

When this life is over and you stand before your Creator to give an account of your life, all the fleeting things of earth will have no value. Prestige, money, accomplishments and goals we make for ourselves, what will they be worth then?

He is Strong

I relied heavily on prayer for the raising of my children. I knew I did not have the strength or the patience to be the Super-Mom I used to be. I needed to find a way to draw on the unlimited strength, love and wisdom of the Holy Spirit, and put it into action in my everyday life.

I discovered that as I came to the Lord often with my questions, He never tired in giving me helpful parenting advice, solutions to specific problems and answers to my kid's needs. As my faithful coach and counselor, He often reminded me to relax and enjoy my family, not to worry or stress or take things so seriously. As I depended on His divine assistance, I saw many miracles take place in our home, often in answer to specific prayers.

As an example: I had felt badly that I was unable to read to my children due to pain in my jaws which made it difficult to even talk. I wanted to teach them the Bible, read stories to them and teach them all that there is to learn in the great world of reading. I laid out my concerns before the throne of Heaven. Before long my children began to take a great individual interest in reading. Their reading skills were already advanced for their age and improved rapidly.

They would read by themselves for hours each day. They were fascinated with books. Everything that I had wanted to read to them they were now reading on their own! I was amazed to see them growing spiritually as well. As their understanding increased, they became more helpful and concerned for others. Although kids are still kids, and by no means perfect, many of the nagging problems slowly faded into the background.

I am so thankful to Jesus that He not only helps us with the big things, but He also has the love and patience to help us with the small things. He is never too busy to get involved with our everyday problems. So many times we struggle needlessly because we think that we should be able to handle things on our own, or we think that a problem is too small to take to the Lord for help. Proverbs 3:5 says, *"In all your ways acknowledge Him and He will make your paths straight."*

Sometimes it's easier to trust God and depend on him for the big things than it is to trust Him for the little things. I know I need His help for the major crises and decisions, but the little things I feel are *my* problem. So I carry the weights and struggle along. After all, why would such a big God care about such small details?

As I stopped to think about it, I was amazed at the great care and attention God put into the smallest of His creations. From the perfect social structure of an ant colony to the precision of a single cell, God's attention to details is plainly evident.

In my home we watch a lot of animal documentaries. They are not only educational, but often fascinating. Each kind of animal, reptile, bird, and insect has their own unique style of courtship, mating, nesting, etc. Many have complex social structures, or intricate nesting designs. Each baby, from the elephant to the honey bee, is raised in an environment marvelously suited to its needs.

All nature, moving with activity and bustling with life, survives because God cares about details. God's creation moves with balance and harmony. Surely this problem I am carrying is not too small for Him. He is my father; He is tuned in to my needs. He knows better than I do how to handle it. I must simply trust Him.

Life Goes On

Little by little we began to get involved in Christian ministry again. Despite our weaknesses, our situation was fairly stable. We also felt it was a special time to train our children and strengthen our bond as a family. Our children had done some performing before, and we called their group "The Sunshine Singers." Now we felt they were old enough to take it to the next level. For two months Daniel practiced with them for one or two hours a day. All this work paid off in a lively Christmas show of singing and dancing.

Throughout December of 2002, we had shows booked nearly every day. We performed for schools, hospitals, senior citizens homes, and even at the George R. Brown Convention Center of Houston for 12,000 people. The kids loved it, and their enthusiasm showed brightly in their work and fun. It was a wonderful and fulfilling Christmas. Through our shows, we were able to bring to many people the joyful message of Christmas.

Shortly after this, we began working with a team to establish a center for producing Christian educational videos. Daniel is well trained and talented in audio-video production. He had worked in this kind of ministry in previous years. This was the perfect opportunity for us; enabling Daniel to feel challenged and needed again.

Drawing on my previous experience doing clown shows in Taiwan, and my years of teaching and entertaining children, I began a clown business to help support our ministry. The schedule was good for me. I cared for my children during the week, and did clown shows for birthday parties and other events on the week-ends.

My business was good, and I became fairly well-known as "Miss Sunshine, the Clown." I enjoyed entertaining children. My clown shows included a comedy/magic show, music and games, face-painting, and balloon sculpting—from tiny animals to giant cartoon characters, and everything in-between. Before long I had a following of little fans that loved and adored their favorite Miss Sunshine.

As our Center became more established, I also got more involved with the management aspects of the ministry. It was good for me to feel useful again. I was so excited about our work, that much of the time I was able to keep my mind focused on something positive, and push to the side my constant and continuing battle with pain and fatigue.

In spite of the active life I was living, I was still struggling very hard with my health. At times, pain would overcome me, and all I could do was rest in bed for days at a time. So I would pray—pray for our ministry, for our church, for my children and for my friends in need. It was a joy to my heart to see the many answers to my prayers during my times of weakness.

Yet, it was also very frustrating to be so weak when there was so much to be done. I often became weary and discouraged with my constant struggle. Daniel faced similar frustrations, as his health limited his abilities also. He would push himself too hard, or do something that required him to bend down. This would aggravate the tumor, and cause a lot of pain which would last for days.

In spite of our afflictions, we forged ahead, and the Lord worked on our behalf. It was a challenging time, yet fulfilling. I often reflected on the scriptures, *"My grace is sufficient for you, for my power is made perfect in weakness"* (2 Corinthians 12:9). *"Those who hope in the Lord will renew their strength"* (Isaiah 40:31). It was a time of spiritual growth, as I relied heavily on the Lord's power to sustain me day by day.

Chapter Nine

BROKEN DREAMS

One fateful day in the spring of 2004, my body completely gave out. I couldn't get up anymore. I had constant severe pain all over my body. Every muscle ached and burned intensely, while stronger, localized pains became much more difficult to deal with. I was so exhausted and weak that even to lift my arm or roll over in bed seemed a challenging feat. The few steps to the bathroom and back were so hard on me, it would take several hours to recover, and for the pain to subside enough that I could relax and rest. I could hardly eat or digest anything at all.

My nervous system was also totally shot. The slightest thing would trigger a feeling of panic. Instantly my nerves would go on fire, and a painful, burning, tingling feeling would shoot out all over my body, like hot oil being injected through my nerves. This would last for hours, and was extremely difficult to cope with.

If anyone raised their voice, if my children started to argue, if there was any loud sound, startling news, or even a phone ringing, it could trigger this painful stress response. I had to distance myself from everyone and everything. I couldn't hear about work, ministry, or even the domestic comings and goings of my own home. I had to be fully protected from even the slightest stress, as my physical and mental condition was too weak to handle it.

I no longer had any reserves of strength or anything else my body needed to recover. The weeks leading up to this had been very busy. I was surviving on a steady supply of caffeine and Tylenol, and pushing myself on in spite of the constant pain and fatigue. I was tired of being ill and did all I could to ignore it. I was proud of my accomplishments and wanted so badly to keep up with the goals I set for myself. Not yet understanding the chronic condition from which I was suffering, I was unaware of how fragile I was or the dangers of such overexertion, till it was too late.

As the days dragged into weeks, then slowly turned into months, my condition was unchanged as I lay completely bedridden. Each time I tried to get up and do things I felt had to be done, my strength simply would not allow it. When I would finally have some energy to get out of bed, by the time I had managed to get dressed and brush my hair, I was completely exhausted again and forced back to bed by the terrible pain. It was a difficult adjustment for me to be so totally disabled. I'd always been such a strong, active, and sociable personality. I want to help everyone, and be involved in everything. Now, life as I knew it had come to a stop.

In order to counter the depressing feeling of being isolated for so long, I would lay on a cot outside for hours each day, soaking up the rich colors of spring. We lived on a large property bordering a forested area that was often filled with the joyful song of birds. The clear blue of the sky and the vibrant green of the trees overhead had a soothing effect on my body, mind and spirit.

After much testing, I was eventually diagnosed with fibromyalgia-syndrome, a life-long and often debilitating condition. This came as a devastating shock. After two years of illness, I had already begun to suspect this as the cause, but I had kept this fear carefully buried in the hidden areas of my mind where I dared not to go. I had seen my mother suffer with fibromyalgia for 25 years. For as long as I could remember she was usually weak and sick.

During the last two years, as I battled the nearly constant pain, I had held to the belief that this was all part of a long, slow recovery from the cancer. It was just a matter of time before I would get well again and have my life back. Now, while I was totally bedridden, I was suddenly faced with the realization that maybe this wasn't going away. My mind battled a torrent of questions and fears as I realized that I could be sick for the rest of my life.

"This can't be happening to me! I am too young! My children are too young! How can I be a good mother? How can I tell my husband that his wife is an invalid?" I felt my whole life, all my dreams and hopes for the future, come crashing down. A suffocating depression settled over me.

I would later understand more fully that many people, at the onset of chronic illness or disability, experience this kind of depression as a natural part of the *grieving* process. Yes, it is a form of grieving – for the loss of my previous life and the woman that I knew, a death of the old me, as well as a loss of all that I had planned, hoped or wished for the future. Everything was gone, and in its place was only uncertainty and pain.

Fighting Through Depression

Depression came over me like a thick dark cloud. Despairing thoughts surrounded me night and day. No matter how much I wanted to have faith, I found myself unable to conquer the giants of despair that loomed over me. I had always been taught to look for the silver lining, the ray of hope even in the midst of seemingly hopeless situations. But now that the night had closed in so black around me, I couldn't find any flicker of hope.

I remember many times crying out to the Lord to deliver me from this depression. Try as I might, I did not have the strength to will my mind into positive thinking. It seemed no matter what I did, or how hard I tried, I could not overcome it. At times like this I prayed, "Lord, hold onto me, when I am too weak even to hold onto You. Just carry me through this storm. Help me find joy again in my life."

The great psalmist, David, understood all too well the travail and vexation of spirit that overwhelms us when such a flood of sorrow engulfs our soul. He wrote,

"Save me, O God; for the waters have come up to my neck. I sink in miry depths, where there is no foothold. I have come into the deep waters; the floods engulf me. I am worn out calling for help; my throat is parched. My eyes fail looking for my God.

"Do not let the floodwaters engulf me, or the depths swallow me up, or the pit close its mouth over me. Answer me, O LORD, out of the goodness of your love; in your great mercy turn to me." (Psalm 69: 1-3, 15-16)

There were times when the tempest of depression threatened to engulf me. The night became so dark around me that I couldn't feel God's presence near me. I knew He was there, somewhere, but why was He now so distant from me at the time when I needed Him most? I saw myself reaching, feeling, grasping out into the air, searching for His love and strength, but finding nothing.

Then, in answer to my deepest prayer, I heard His tender voice:

"The reason you cannot see Me or reach Me there in front of you, is because I am right here behind you. My strong arms are around you, holding you from behind. All you have to do is lay your head back on My shoulder and rest. Don't reach, don't struggle, and don't try so hard to find My presence; just rest in My everlasting arms."

I knew then that He was with me. Even at the times when I couldn't see or feel Him, He was there all along, supporting and holding me. I had previously thought that I was the one who had to hold onto God. Yet, in reality, it was God who was holding onto me. Though at times I felt I could not find Him, nor did I even have the strength to hold-on to anything at all, I did not need to fear. God would not let me go. I needed only to rest in His arms.

My experience, though, was far from passive. I found that my fight against depression was a daily battle of will. I had to make a conscious choice to not give up, and to praise God even if I didn't feel like it, to smile when I wanted to cry, to look for the good and beauty in life when all had become so bleak. I had every right to be miserable, to wallow in self pity, to voice my pain and vent my anger on the world around me, or to shut myself off in silent grief. But that would only hurt the ones I loved.

For the sake of my family I could not allow myself to give in to this depression. My being sick for so long already had taken a toll on them. My husband was taking this very hard. I could see that my illness was tearing him apart, and I could not bear to add to His pain. For his sake I had to find a way to overcome.

I knew my depression had several causes:

- Physical – caused by the constant pain and exhaustion
- Mental – adjusting to this state of disability
- Emotional – as my mind was weighed down with fear and negativity at the point when I was weakest

It would seem that all the cards were stacked against me. Who could be happy under such circumstances?

Although this battle was long and hard, with no quick easy victory, I did learn various techniques that were a great help to me. Though the clouds seemed ever present, the storm surges came in waves. I had to learn to ride each wave as it came. Sometimes it just meant holding on for dear life until that wave passed. *"He who stands firm to the end will be saved"* (Mathew 24:13).

My lifesaver was to take one promise from the Bible and hold onto it. I would repeat that promise to myself again and again.—Promises such as, *"My grace is sufficient for you, for My power is made perfect in weakness"* (2 Corinthians 12:9), and many other wonderful promises. I was determined not to give in to this depression. Like

Peter, I had to keep my eyes on Jesus and not look at the waves, or I'd sink into the ocean of despair. Many times when I felt that I was sinking, I'd repeat the verse, *"When my heart is overwhelmed, lead me to the rock that is higher than I"* (Psalm 61:2 KJV).

The Bible says, *"You are from God and have overcome them, because the one who is in you is greater than the one who is in the world"* (1 John 4:4.) I remember my grandfather saying, "There is a power to hold you up, that is stronger than all the powers that hold you down."

It is impossible to overstate the power of holding onto a single promise from God's Word and claiming it for yourself. There is power in His words. *"The words I have spoken unto you are spirit and they are life"* (John 6:63). It is not necessary to be a Bible scholar and know hundreds of verses by memory. Just start with one, and repeat it line by line until it becomes a part of you.

Don't Stand Alone

I learned another valuable strategy in my fight against depression. Once again, I had to seek out the help of others. For a long time I had tried to muddle through by myself, but with very little progress. I was barely surviving—holding my head above water, but not overcoming. Through prayer, praise and scriptures I was taking a stand, but it was just not enough to stand alone.

Jesus wanted me to be happy. So, as a good doctor, He gave me specific orders. He said:

"When this wave of depression comes over you, if you cannot pull yourself out of it in a reasonable amount of time with the

means that I have given you, then you need to ask someone to pray for you. This is very humbling for you, I know, but it's good for you. It brings humility. It draws you close to others. It helps them to see what you are going through, and to understand and love you more. It increases the bond of unity between you. My spirit dwells in love and unity. This is a powerful, spiritual force that will support you."

I experienced myself many times the truth of the Bible verse, *"Two are better than one… if one falls down, his friend can help him up."* (Ecclesiastes 4:9, 10). This was when my real progress started. To ask for help "as often as I needed" sometimes meant every day. I was blessed to have several close friends that I could confide in, who were also a spiritual strength in my life, and who were more than happy to be there for me. I didn't like to talk to Daniel about it, as I knew this would weigh heavily on him.

After several hours, if I could not pull out of a severe bout of gloom, I would call a friend. Somehow, talking about it and praying together had a healing effect, and made me feel better. Eventually the battles got easier and less frequent.

It is humbling to be in a position where it is necessary to receive help from others. But I have learned that by opening myself up to receive from them, a kindness is shared, and God's blessings are multiplied.

Many people are afraid to accept help from others. Perhaps they feel it will lessen their dignity or self-worth to be dependent on others. But sometimes God puts us in just such a position, so that the humility brought forth in our lives will deepen our relationships with those around us. It also gives those who are helping us the opportunity to reach out in love, and to receive a blessing of their own.

Chapter Ten

TOTAL TRANSFORMATION

Then one day the miracle of deliverance from this depression was fulfilled. The following is my journal entry for June 24, 2004.

A wonderful miracle has come over me. I have come to a point of perfect peace about my condition, and the dark clouds of depression have lifted. I started thinking about the many great men and women who have carried on in spite of terrible handicaps or disabilities. I remembered reading about a missionary who was bound to a wheelchair, but still carried on a wonderful ministry overseas, touching countless lives.

I also thought about the missionary family I knew of who had a deaf child. Their work with this child prompted them to start a ministry for the deaf, helping thousands of deaf children and adults in India.

Then the words of Dr. Irwin Moon played over and over in my mind all day. After learning that he would be permanently blind, he prayed, "Lord, I accept this talent of blindness from Thee. Help me to use it for Thy glory." Then he went on to develop the Moon Alphabet for the blind, enabling thousands of blind people to read scriptures for the first time.

Dear Jesus, You have given me this handicap. Help me to use it somehow for Your glory. I accept Your will for my life, even though I do not understand it. I yield to You and find great freedom, joy, peace and contentment. So many other people have overcome disabilities much greater than mine. Look at Fanny Crosby and Helen Keller. Lord, if they could be content and serve you, then surely I can.

Help me, Lord, to look at what I have and what I can do, and not at what I don't have and can't do. Help me to be thankful for the life I live, the husband I love, and the children we share. I have so many blessings.

I cannot promise that I will be strong or always positive, but Lord, I yield My life to You now. If You know that I can serve You better with this weakness, then take this broken body and make it a vessel of Your love. I surrender to You my will, my plans, my future and my dreams. Those are the hardest to let go of. I give it all to You. Make something wonderful, as only You can. Thank You for the peace and joy I find in yielding to Your will. There is no room for fear. I know You would do me no wrong.

I was filled with an amazing sense of peace and purpose. It was as though a breath of life had been breathed back into me, bringing with it a total transformation, a renewing of my heart and mind. And just like that... my depression was lifted.

I later spoke with a woman who leads a fibromyalgia support group. She said, "You cannot begin the healing process until you get over the grieving process. For many people it takes three to five years to get past this grieving stage, to where they can accept their condition, and learn to be content, in order to go on from there toward recovery." I marveled at the miracle Jesus had done in my life, that after only three months I had found this place of healing and peace.

The light of God's love had penetrated the deep darkness and illuminated my heart as the sunlight breaks forth in the morning. I meditated on these words, *"For thou wilt light my candle: the LORD my God will enlighten my darkness"* (Psalm 18:28 KJV). *"If I say, Surely the darkness shall cover me; even the night shall be light about me."* (Psalm 139: 11 KJV)

The Faith of a Child

After this, I was able to share this new outlook on life with my children, and help them to adjust and gain peace about my situation. They often asked, "Why did God let you get sick? Why doesn't God heal you?" They carried a lot of weight, both physically and emotionally, because of my illness. It was important for them to understand.

I sat them all down for a talk, and told them many stories of people who overcame great handicaps.— Specifically, stories of how God used their handicaps to accomplish some greater purpose. I brought out several important points in my discussion with them.

- God has a plan and purpose for our lives. He has a good reason why He allowed this to happen.

- We don't have to understand everything right now. We just have to take it by faith that someday we will understand. Then we'll see that God's way is perfect.

- We can look at others who have overcome great handicaps, and marvel at what God was able to do through them.

- If others could still serve God, in spite of their difficulties, so can we.

- If they could be happy and content with their lives, we can also.

- We can count our blessings. Mommy's not crippled or blind. Things aren't so bad.

- The children will have to take on more responsibility to make up for Mommy's weaknesses. This will make them stronger and more mature.

The kids took up the challenge beautifully. They accepted my explanation with simple, childlike faith, and took it as their responsibility to help take care of me and keep our family functional. I am so proud of them, that they have matured and grown so much through all of this.

It's difficult for children when their mommy is sick. They want to come jump on the bed, tell me about their exciting day, tell on their brothers and sisters, or complain about school. I felt so bad always having to tell them, "Please be quiet. Mommy's not feeling well. Don't bump the bed. No hugs now. Tell me later." I wanted them to be able to come to me, and sometimes I could handle it. But when my pain was most severe, even the slightest movement was unbearable. How could they know when to approach me, without me always having to talk about how sick I was?

One day we came up with a brilliant idea that solved this problem, and greatly eased the tension for both me and the kids. Different colored flags, (a scarf hung by my bed), gave them a clear signal as to how I was feeling and what they were allowed to do. A white flag meant: mommy's feeling okay; now is a good time to visit. A yellow flag meant: mommy's not feeling well; you can come in if you're very quiet and still. The red flag meant: mommy's very sick; you can pray for her and blow a kiss at the door, but don't come in or try to talk to her.

The children liked this system and responded respectfully. When I rested outside, they would even bring me my flag to tie onto my chair. Sometimes they would tie the scarf to the outside of my bedroom door to remind each other to be quiet and not disturb me. I was impressed by their thoughtfulness and concern.

Although I could not do activities with them, I was thankful to see our bond of love growing stronger in our one-on-one times together when they would come to visit and talk with me. Often I found they were remarkably sensitive to my feelings, attuned to my needs and full of compassion. At times they would question, "Why did God let you be sick?" Then we would talk about all the good things that have come into our lives through this time, and remind ourselves of all of God's blessings.

Now I can look back and see how much they've learned as a result of my weakness. My children have had to be more responsible and independent, learning to cook at a young age, wash laundry, and carry the bulk of the work load around the house. At times other parents comment in amazement at how many things my children have learned to do and how mature and capable they are. I am comforted to see how my weakness has worked for good in their lives.

My daughter, Chalsey, at only 11 years of age, wrote this poem for me as a gift for my birthday. I marvel as I see the beauty and wisdom which she expresses in her writing, way beyond her years. (Note: in Christian writings a cross is often used to denote our sufferings or the sacrifices we make in our service for God.)

Your Cross is Your Crown

Sometimes it seems the cross you bear,
May just be too much.
But when you come to the Lord in prayer,
He gives His magical touch.

He says to you, "It's okay my love."
And helps when you're feeling down.
He says, "Pick up the cross My love,
Because it's actually your crown."

"This cross a crown? How can it be?"
"Beauty from ashes." He says.
"You will see what I mean someday,
When I place this crown on your head."

"After you've passed through the fire and flood,
Though it seems you almost drown.
You'll come out a gentle soul and say,
'My cross really is my crown'."

I love you Mom! Happy Birthday!
Chalsey, 11 years old.

A Mother's Influence

This also got me thinking about my mother, and the influence that she had on me. For as long as I can remember, my mother was always struggled with her health. During my younger years growing up in Asia, I remember having very loving and dedicated full-time teachers and guardians, for whom I still feel the greatest gratitude. But Mom was always there for us in the background. She organized our school and made sure we were well looked after. She was always there to run to when I needed someone to talk to, or a shoulder to cry on.

She was always positive, cheerful, and full of faith. She taught me to see God's hand in all things, to turn to Him for help, and to follow His plan for my life. She also taught me to be compassionate to those in need, to look past outward appearances, and to understand people's hearts. She never placed much importance on material wealth or success. She had a deeper, richer sense of values which was clearly evident in her life.

She coped amazingly well with her condition, or at least she hid it well from us kids. It was not until the last few years that I began to understand what she went through. Until recently, very little was known about fibromyalgia. As with most FMS sufferers at that time, the doctors were unable to diagnose her problems. This added to the weight of her plight, as she struggled to cope with an illness that "didn't exist."

Although she did go through severe depression at various stages of her illness, her overall attitude towards her life has been surprisingly positive and full of faith. It was her faith that was instrumental in helping me to adjust to my condition. She had learned to see her weakness as her strength. She depended heavily on God in her daily life, and as a result, she carried the peace and power that comes only from a life grafted in Christ. This had a powerful effect on me as I was growing up.

Chapter Eleven

GRACE TO ENDURE

Regardless of how strong we think we are or try to be, the effects of long-term illness can be difficult to cope with. Reserves of courage are depleted and patience wears thin. Coupled with the pain of the moment, is the helplessness of not seeing any end in sight. During the ongoing months, as I struggled to adjust to the new life I had so suddenly found myself in, I experienced a wide range of emotions, guilt, and frustrations as the reality of my condition confronted me day after day.

I had been freed from the monsters of fear and depression that at first had overwhelmed me. I had gained a definite peace regarding my condition, and this change was evident in the way I now viewed myself and my illness. Yet this type of severe ongoing illness naturally brings periodic waves of discouragement and weariness, caused by the prolonged physical and mental exhaustion. Now as I learned to depend on Him for my strength, I found a daily renewal of that miracle.

I spent countless days in bed with only Jesus and my prayer journal for company. As I recorded my prayers and

His answers, these became such a tremendous source of strength and joy to me. No matter how hard the trials were that I faced, His words never failed to bring me the comfort I needed. They are not empty words, offering false hopes and promises. Time and again I saw the fulfillment of these messages come to pass in my life. *"My comfort in my suffering is this: Your promise preserves my life"* (Psalm 119:50). At times I wondered how God could be so patient with me. I didn't like that I was always so needy. It was hard for me to be so dependent. But His response to me was kind and understanding.

"Don't be afraid to come back to Me to get a new dose of My strength for the day. I am always ready to give again. When your faith is low, when your courage runs dry, when the mountains before you seem insurmountable, when your strength fails and your frame is weak, I am always there, always strong, always ready to lift up your head and smile kindly."

"Your affliction is the binding cord that draws Me near. Whenever you feel weak and weary, and in need of My comfort and strength, I will be nearest when you need Me most. This is the cord of our love. I am holding you closest when your human frame is weak."

He has given me such a great wealth of comfort to draw on that I feel almost spoiled. The treasures I have gained from my pain were worth far more than anything this world can offer. I understood the meaning of 2 Corinthians 12:9,10. *"Therefore I will boast all the more gladly about my weaknesses, so that Christ's power may rest on me. That is why, for Christ's sake, I delight in weakness... For when I am weak, then I am strong."*

Living with Fibromyalgia

In an attempt to stay somewhat connected to life around me, I made it a goal, once a day, to get up from my bed and sit for a while in the living room and talk with family or friends, even if only for a few minutes. In the afternoon, if I was well enough, I made the effort to walk to the end of the driveway and back.

Even the simplest of tasks posed a challenge for me. Taking a shower would use up a whole days' worth of strength. Sweeping my bedroom could take two weeks to recover from; folding laundry was a killer. I had to depend on others for everything. Many days I needed the help of a massage just to be able to sit up or get out of bed. My son became very good at it, even renting books from the library on massage therapy. He was so kind and helpful.

Taking a hot bath had amazing therapeutic power. It was the only thing that could bring relief from the pain in my nerves and enable me to relax. But the strain of dressing and walking back to my room afterwards would quickly undo any measure of relief I had achieved. The only solution was when I could just wrap in a robe and be carried from the bath directly to my bed; which could afford me a few blessed hours of comfortable rest.

Another life-saver for me was having a very comfortable folding lawn chair, in which I would recline for hours on the porch, taking in the beauty of nature. When I was feeling well enough, my husband would take me to the park, where I could rest in my chair and enjoy a change of scenery. This time outdoors was an essential element in my recovery process. It was soothing on my nerves and helped to relieve my depression.

Later as I began to recover a little, I would have my chair placed next to a flowerbed by the house. Pruning a few branches and pulling a few weeds provided a sort of therapy for me. From the busy life I once knew, I now had a pace so slow that I was literally watching the flowers grow. I knew each plant so well, noticed every new budding twig, and smiled with each new bloom.— Observing the miracle of life unfold before my eyes as the growth of spring touched my own heart as well.

Eventually a comfortable electric wheel chair was donated to me, enabling me to get out of the house sometimes and be with my family. My kids loved it, always wanting to get on the back for a ride, or race me down the path. Suddenly my little girl was always too tired to walk, or had a sore leg, any excuse to ride with mommy.

I was thankful for the times when I had a little strength to get up and move around a bit. Though still feeling sick and achy, this was considered a good day, and was a rare blessing. I could walk around a little and do a few things I needed to do, in spite of the nagging pain and fatigue. The problem was that when I finally could get up, I would easily do too much; the slightest thing would have me bedridden again.

While in bed, I was happy if I could at least do mild brain work to distract myself. I could read a book, write a letter, talk to a friend, or pray for others. If I lay still enough, I could keep the pain under control and reasonably tolerable.

I often had to have a distraction to focus on in order to cope. I would watch a mild TV show or a calm movie rerun to keep my mind off the pain, or else the tension would quickly cause the pain to escalate out of control.

I sometimes felt guilty watching movies in the middle of the day, when there was so much to be done, or watching TV all night, but it provided some relief, and helped the difficult hours to pass more quickly.

When the pain was most severe I needed one hundred percent concentration just to hold on and endure. I needed to be perfectly still in a dark room with no noise or distractions. I would concentrate on breathing slowly and trying to remain calm, though often I could not keep from crying.

At times when the pain was so unbearable, just the thought of enduring through a long day of such intense pain would overwhelm me with despair. I had to set small goals for myself in order to be able to bear it. I would break the day into three-hour segments. I'd pray, "Lord, help me to make it to 3:00. Give me the grace to hold on a little longer. Help the time to pass quickly." Then there was a feeling of relief when 3:00 came around, like, "I made it! I survived this far!" I felt so grateful that I passed one time marker in my day, and with that came a glimmer of hope that I could then make it to 6:00.

I was so thankful for the prayers of my family and friends and support from my church during this time. They carried me through when I was too weak to even pray for myself. I could feel the difference when they would pray: a touch of relief, a few blessed hours of sleep, or a magical retreat in my Saviors arms—some small miracle to get me through the long hours. It was not an instant physical healing; instead, He gave me the grace to endure, the peace to trust, and a little rest in His arms to get me through the storm.

During such times of dire need, Jesus touched me with several out-of-this-world, supernatural experiences and visions, where my soul could soar and be free high above this body of suffering. Such a treasure is beyond worth! I have seen, like the old song says, "It will be worth it all, when we see Jesus; life's trials will seem so small, when we see Christ." There is nothing in this life that can compare with the wonders of His love.

At times I felt I was being pushed beyond the limits of my human endurance, but often that is the very place where miracles happen. In my times of greatest suffering, I felt the greatest measure of God's comfort and presence. It is when we are stretched beyond ourselves and our human limitations that we step into the vast greatness of God's power. Such total dependency on Him is what makes it possible for Him to do great things in us.

I would soon learn this concept on a whole new level, when after a while my eyes also fell prey to fibromyalgia's paralyzing grip. I was no longer able to read, or watch TV. I couldn't work on my writing or help my child with a homework question. Even just a few seconds to look at and dial a phone number would result in hours of eye pain and headaches.

I was told by a specialist that this problem was the result of my illness, therefore not correctable by glasses or treatment. What's more, he could not tell me if I would ever regain the use of my eyes again. Though I was not officially going blind, the affect it had was similar. I had lost the ability to use my sight in any working capacity. My eye muscles could not handle the strain of sustained focus or eye movement.

I struggled to suppress the fears of what the implications of this would be on my life. Being bedridden most of the time already, the use of my eyes was all I had to keep me occupied or feeling a little useful. Now I could do nothing but lie there; a prisoner in my body, shackled to my bed and cut off from the world. I could bear the pain bravely, but I could not bear the boredom, the feeling of uselessness, the frustration of not being able to contribute in any purposeful way.

At that time a friend came to visit me. I confided in her my desperate need to feel useful again. If I was to be so incapacitated, I had to find a way to adjust to this role and regain my joy of living, so that this sickness would not weigh so heavily on my spirit. Together we prayed for God to intervene and open a way for me, either with a miracle of healing or with a miracle of renewed grace and faith.

The next day I came across an audio book, "Action Through Prayer". As I listened I felt a supernatural infusion of inspiration and purpose. I felt a call in my heart that God had more for me to do. I was being presented with a challenge to put God to the test and see how much could really be accomplished through prayer. This was an opportunity to stand as an official representative for my family, friends and those in need, to bring their petitions before the courts of Heaven and see what God would do. From the quiet of my room, far from the distractions of the busy day, here was my place to work. God was close to me there, giving me strength in the spirit which I lacked in the flesh.

Throughout the months that followed I was often amazed at the many miracles the Lord did as a result of the ministry of prayer He had called me to. On every side I was seeing real, substantial, physical changes where God's power was at work doing what I could not do. I saw positive effects my prayers had on my home, family, friends, and our ministry. I was thrilled at what could be accomplished in my quiet hours of seeming inactivity. Though all around me was still and quiet, I had discovered my place of active service by working within another realm. Yes, it really was possible to work through prayer.

Fear and Anger

"Degenerative and irreversible!" The words echoed in my head as I cried in secret. For a long time I managed to stay cheerful in spite of my weaknesses. Then my health took a turn for the worse, and I developed another condition that further limited my ability. I did not know how to tell my husband about this new diagnosis. I was too ashamed to tell him.

I felt as though the last of my womanhood had been stripped from me. Being completely disabled by my illness, I already could not care for my husband or take care of my children, and now this. It seemed my body was deteriorating irreversibly.

I suddenly found myself facing down the monsters of a new fear. I did not doubt my husband's love and loyalty, but I deeply doubted myself. *How long would he stay interested in me? Will I become only a burden to him? Isn't it only a matter of time before he will finally get tired of me and want a 'real' wife? After all, men have basic needs.* I felt like a total failure as a wife and a mother, with nothing left to give. It is difficult to express how all these things were so totally degrading to the little self-esteem I had left.

The haunting voice lingered in my mind, as though telling him, "I'm sorry, but the model you purchased is defective and irreparable. It's time to upgrade to a new model."

I could just imagine all the young, healthy, pretty women that were bound to catch his eye, while I was only a burdensome weight, a bedridden invalid.- Wouldn't he eventually want to be free of me? Wouldn't it even be unfair, selfish, and cruel of me to hang on to him? After all, he deserved someone better than me.

While I loved him too much to bear the thought of losing him; equally painful was the thought of the life that he would be missing out on if I continued to weigh him down. I wanted more for him than that. I'd had such dreams when we married. Looking at him with fond admiration, I'd cherished the thought of being the woman that would stand beside him as he journeyed through life, and be there to support him while he pursued his passions. Where was that woman now? What had become of the life we had dreamed of sharing together?

Despair overwhelmed me, and, for the first time in my life, I found myself really angry with God.

"How could you do this to me?! You have already taken everything I have. Will you take my husband away as well? If you truly are a loving God, how could you allow all this? How much can one person take? I'm too young to be going through this! I'm only 29 years old, but already I feel like an old woman!"

The struggle of fear and anger raged through my mind for some time before I finally worked up the courage to talk to Daniel, tell him of my recent diagnosis and what I was going through.

His reaction was calm, caring, and surprisingly soothing to my troubled heart. He assured me that he would love me always, that our love was deeper and stronger than circumstances. He told me softly, "We took an oath, remember? *'To love and to cherish, in sickness and in health'.* We're in this together no matter what. You know, I'd rather have a little bit of you than a whole lot of somebody else."

Somehow, just talking about it, and hearing his expressions of love, went a long way in helping to dispel the fears that had so strongly come over me. Whatever challenge life presented us with; we could bear it, if we faced it together.

For a while I had been angry at God, I hardly wanted to talk to Him much less listen. In my moment of despair I had vented words and feelings of frustration and anger towards Him, blaming Him for my heartache. I had questioned His methods and His motives. I felt He was cruel and unfair to allow so much evil to befall me.

But how could I stay mad at God? He had been the one thing I could hold onto. His love had been my strength, and I needed His words of love and comfort more now than ever. Yet after I had rejected Him and spoken so badly to Him, would He still speak to me? Would He forgive my lack of faith? Was it considered a sin to reject Him in this way? Or would He understand?

Yes, He was as near as ever. His reply did not delay in coming to me and was filled with compassion and kindness. He knows our human frame and understands our weaknesses. He reminded me again of the beautiful passage in the Bible:

The Lord is compassionate and gracious; slow to anger and abounding in love. For as high as the heavens are above the earth, so great is His love for those who fear Him. As a father has compassion on his children, so the Lord has compassion on those who fear Him. For He knows how we are formed, He remembers that we are dust (Psalm 103:8, 11, 13-14).

Again I meditated on this comforting thought which I had read years ago. "Jesus has great compassion on those who find the cross of their suffering too heavy. He too fell under the weight of His own cross, and had to be helped by a passerby."

Slowly I regained my peace with God and found in Him the strength and comfort I so desperately needed. I had to come once again to that point of surrender in my life, where I could place all my fears into His loving hands and leave them there, knowing that He would not fail to care for Me.

Now, after all these years, it is easy to see how He has been true to me. He has brought me through every storm. Gradually my health has improved, and those fears which had seemed so real to me then, are now only a fleeting memory of the past.

Now going on twenty years of marriage, Daniel and I are still as in-love as the day we married, actually, even more so. Through all the hardships our love has only deepened. Daniel still romances me with flowers and chocolates, and takes me out on dates to spend quality time together. This love we share has been the single greatest gift God has given me in my life, permeating and bringing such rich sweetness into all our shared experiences.

To Bare the Unbearable

With so many extreme hardships one after the other, I had found myself questioning the oft used phrase, "God does not give us burdens greater than we are able to bear." With what we had been through, who wouldn't wonder?

Not more than I can bear? Doesn't He know my weak state? I crumple like a squashed flower under the weights of such burdens. The giants that have come against me are truly more than I can handle. The pressures placed upon me, indeed are above anything my human strength can bear. How could a loving God stand by and watch while we are crushed by an unbearable load?

But as I look closer into the heart of God, I see it a new way. I understand that it is in this very phrase we find the flaw in this way of thinking, and through it we also discover the secret of its meaning.

The truth is: *you* can't handle it. Yet, in those times when life is so *unbearable* and we *can't* handle it, we can find divine *"grace to help us in our time of need"* (Hebrews 4:16). He said, *"My grace is sufficient for you"* (2 Corinthians 12:9). He does not ask us to bear the unbearable. He says. *"Come to me, all you who are weary and burdened, and I will give you rest"* (Mathew 11:28). He will lift our burdens. He will bear our cross. He and I can bear it together.

This is the miracle of dying grace. Christ in us. He came to take our burdens on Himself. He came to get involved in our lives, and to be our strength. It is not when we are strong that we discover His power; it is when we are weak, when we are insufficient. *"Not that we are sufficient of ourselves... but our sufficiency is of God"* (2 Corinthians 3:5 KJV).

I have personally been in many unbearable circumstances, where I felt that the pain and fatigue, the mental and emotional stress, the fear and despair, were more than I could bear. But never once has Jesus failed me. Never once has He left me alone. There has never been a time when His grace was not *sufficient* for me. I have leaned on Him, depended on Him, and when I could do nothing else, I have fallen, helpless, into His strong arms. He *is* strong enough. He *does* care.

It is at that moment when human strength is gone, that I discover the reliability of His strength. It is only when we come to the end of ourselves that we can truly know the sufficiency of Christ. It is in this dependency on Him that we truly *know* Him in us. *"Christ in you, the hope of glory"* (Colossians 1:27).

In this, then, is our hope and strength. From this truth came the words of Paul, through terrible suffering and tribulation: *"That is why, for Christ's sake, I delight in weakness... For when I am weak, then I am strong."* (2 Corinthians 12:9).

We are weak, but He is strong. We are insufficient, but His grace *is* sufficient. Our troubles are unbearable, but He will bear them for us. *"Surely He took up our infirmities and carried our sorrows"* (Isaiah 53:4).

Following is one of my favorite passages of scripture: Psalms 116:1-8.

1. I love the LORD, for He heard my voice; He heard my cry for mercy.

2. Because He turned His ear unto me, I will I call on Him as long as I live.

3. The cords of death entangled me, the anguish of the grave came upon me; I was overcome by trouble and sorrow.

4. Then I called on the name of the LORD; O LORD, save me.

5. The Lord is gracious and righteous; our God is full of compassion.

6. The LORD protects the simplehearted; when I was in need, He saved me.

7. Be at rest once more, O my soul, for the LORD has been good to you.

8. For You, O Lord, have delivered my soul from death, my eyes from tears, my feet from stumbling.

Chapter Twelve

PRISON OF PAIN
OR PAVILION OF PEACE

My priorities, my ideas, and my whole outlook on life were changing. I used to be so accomplishment-oriented. My To-Do list had been important to me. They were all things I was so sure had to be done. I had been busy, hurried and pressured with all that I needed to do. Yet now I couldn't do anything at all, not even take care of myself! My whole life, my work, and my To-Do list had suddenly been put on hold, indefinitely.

My first big shock was that life went on without me. The gaps were eventually filled; things slowly adjusted and fell into place. My husband, children and friends stepped in to meet the most demanding needs, while other work was simply left undone, and I had to learn to accept that.

To my surprise, life did not fall apart. Our ministry did not grind to a halt. Amazingly enough, even the sun continued to shine each day without any help from me! All those important things I had needed to do were suddenly not that important anymore. I wondered how I had allowed myself to be put under such pressure before this.

At first my confinement seemed somewhat like a prison sentence, I was so restless with ideas and worries. My normally active personality went through a culture shock as I tried to adjust to prolonged rest in bed. But as I gradually learned to rest in body and mind, a change came over me. My quiet solitude became a sacred blessing, a place of deep and genuine communion with Jesus. The longer I stayed in this place, the further the cares of this world drifted away from me, and the things of Heaven became nearer and clearer. My prison of pain had become a pavilion of peace, with wide open windows looking out over another dimension.

My time of bed rest was no longer boring. In fact, I began to fully enjoy this time, just soaking in Jesus' presence. My relationship with Him became so real and close that I didn't feel alone or lonely. I treasured each moment as I meditated on His Word and learned many new things. It seemed that all I knew was so little compared to the wonders of His knowledge. I felt small and humbled by all that I learned from Him, coupled by an insatiable desire to understand more.

All my accomplishments seemed to be worth so little to me then. All that mattered was Him. Even if all I could do was to lie in bed and praise Him, it was enough. I felt totally complete in Him. In spite of the pain and discomfort, this time had become so special to me that I was actually afraid to lose it. My sickbed had become a blessed sanctuary, giving me glimpses into the Heavenly realm. I wanted to keep this feeling forever.

I struggle still to find words to describe such total bliss. It is *Joy unspeakable and full of glory.* (1 Peter 1:8) It was a love that permeated every fiber of my being, a joy that filled me to overflowing. I remember thinking that this must what Heaven is like, the beauty of which God was giving me a glimpse of here on earth. It was so real, I could touch it, revel in it.

I wondered about what other religions called Nirvana, a state of freedom from pain and suffering, to be one with the universe. What I felt was not the freedom of non-existence. It was real and alive, a complete freedom found in a relationship with God that transcends all our earthly boundaries, with the power to release me from the binds of my suffering, and cause my spirit to soar, to be one with the great God of the universe. This was true and total freedom.

I had nothing at all to offer Him except myself, my love and my praise. Yet, that was all He wanted, and that was all I wanted. As I lay there in my bed unable to move, it might have seemed as if I had nothing. Yet He was more than enough for me. He was my sustenance, my peace, my joy, my purpose, and my all. I had discovered the truth of the saying, "When you have nothing left but Jesus, then you realize that He's all you need."

"Though outwardly we are wasting away, yet inwardly we are being renewed day by day." (2 Corinthians 4:16).

It was then that I slowly penned the following poem as each line flowed from the depths of my heart:

The Truest Strength

I cannot look, I cannot see,
I cannot understand.
I lay myself down helplessly
In the hollow of Thy hand.
The clouds that now encompass me
And seem to block my view,
Are sent by Your unfailing love,
To draw me close to You.

I cease from all my struggling,
I rest from all the strain.
I only live to love You, Lord,
And glorify Thy name.
There is no great achievement now,
No great works done for You,
But somehow in the stillness sweet,
My spirit is renewed.

When pain has overtaken me
And human strength is gone,
Emotions cloud all over me,
The days and nights are long.
I just look up into Your eyes,
And find strength in Your smile.
Your spirit gently comforts me
And holds me through each trial.

And though my body trembles now,

My spirit is at peace,

For I hold to the Master's words

Which cause the storm to cease.

His power stands unfailingly,

His every promise sure.

He gives me faith, He gives me grace

Sufficient to endure.

I lift my heart in praise to You

For all that You have done,

For every battle we have fought,

Each victory we have won!

And though my body pains me still,

My spirit is at peace,

For I have found the Truest Strength,

And in Him is release.

Marie Morrow

Where Your Prayers Have Gone

As a result of my loved ones prayers, I was enveloped in a bubble of grace and comfort. I often felt that it was harder on my husband than it was for me. I had the supernatural peace of God which gave me the grace to endure, but my poor husband had to watch me suffer. As brave and cheery as I tried to be, he knew how severe my pain really was. He watched my body slowly wasting away and he was literally sick with worry for me.

Time after time he prayed his heart out for me. At times he felt he had no tears left to cry. Yet in spite of all his prayers, my condition remained the same. I knew this troubled him deeply. Did it do any good to pray? If it was not God's will or time to heal me, than what was the use in praying?

These questions nagged at him. I felt peace in my heart on the matter, but I did not know how to answer him. I wondered myself, "What good do prayers do, if it is not God's will or time to heal?" Several times I prayed for an answer to this, but received nothing yet.

Then one day I received something extraordinary! It came in the form of a poem. Line by line, I heard the voice in my heart and wrote it down. It expressed exactly the way I felt, and fully addressed my question at the same time. I was amazed at the way God chose to respond. For weeks I had tried unsuccessfully to find an answer to give to my husband. Now it flowed from my pen with simple clarity.

Where Your Prayers Have Gone

Do you want to know where your prayers have gone?
The ones that you prayed last night,
When you poured out your heart before His throne,
And pleaded for help in my plight.

You had prayed so hard that I would be healed.
The answer, it seems, didn't come.
Had He closed His heart to your earnest prayer?
Or doesn't He hear every one?

He gathered your prayers up into His arms,
And mixed them with His own tears,
Creating a mixture of purest Love,
And brought it to ease all my fears.

He came to me in my room last night,
And He tenderly stroked my hair.
He poured the elixir to heal my soul,
In answer to your dearest prayer.

The pain didn't seem so bad just then,
And the night not quite so long.
The joy of His presence that filled my room,
Then filled My heart with its song.

I truly believe I am richly blessed,
As I bask in Heavenly glow.
The treasures I find in affliction's cave
Are more than the richest can know.

Do you want to know where your prayers have gone?
Believe me, they're never in vain.
They return with courage, comfort and faith,
And shower down on me like rain.

So please don't give up in your prayers for me,
Although I'm not healed right away.
He answers your prayers in the way He knows best,
And gives me His grace for today.

Marie Morrow

Such special touches of God's grace sometimes came in new and unexpected ways. Once when I was very ill, Jesus told me that he had given me an Angel of Comfort to be with me during those difficult times. I never saw her face, but through many long days and lonely nights, when the pain was at its worst, I could feel her presence, like a tender mother, stroking my hair and holding me close. It was such a blessed feeling of peace, like a soft, warm aura that enveloped me. I felt as though I lay my head down on her lap, as she softly stroked my head.

Although I could not feel or touch her with my earthly senses, her presence was so tangible and real. Then, in spite of the pain, I found my heart filled with wonder and thankfulness for this special touch from Heaven. One thing I am certain of: God's spiritual realm is not far away from us, just floating around on clouds in Heaven. Angels are here on earth, all around us, to serve, aid, comfort and protect us. We may not be able to see them, but at times we can see or feel the ripples of their effects and know that they are near.

His Healing Hand

Although at the time of writing this I still suffer from fibromyalgia, my story would not be complete if I failed to tell you of the many smaller miracles of healing, the touches of heaven, which have made a big difference in how my condition affects me. Much in the same way as a doctor will prescribe a medicinal remedy for a particularly bothersome symptom, Jesus often gave me touches of His grace to relieve a certain pain or symptom that was causing me distress. So while I have not been fully healed, I have felt His healing on many levels in my life.

Time and time again I have experienced this healing power in answer to prayer. At times, it is a divine touch that brings full and instant relief of my pain, followed by sweet hours of sleep. At other times, it is a healing of that pain or symptom which is the most problematic at the time. More often still, it is the heavenly comfort and grace that fills me with peace and strength to endure. Regardless of how and when He chooses to answer, He does answer. *"God is faithful; He will not let you be tempted beyond what you can bear. But when you are tempted, He will also provide a way out so that you can stand up under it"*(1 Corinthians 10:13).

On one such occasion, I had been awake for hours during the night; the pain was unrelenting. I had borne it as bravely as I could, yet the pain was so hard to bear. Finally, in tears, I woke Daniel up, asking Him to pray for me. He placed his hand on my back and prayed softly. Immediately I felt soft warmth, beginning from his hand, and spreading out all over my body. The pain faded instantly and was gone; it was like a powerful morphine injection, bringing total relief. I fell into a long and peaceful sleep. It was a divine touch of heavenly relief for which I was very thankful.

Stories such as these are so many in my experience. Suffice it to say, God still does miracles today. In fact, were it not for the healing of my painful eye condition I would never have been able to write this book.

So while I could see that this illness was fulfilling a higher purpose in my personal life, part of that purpose was teaching me to lay hold on God's power for my particular need. By this, I was learning the wonderful art of depending deeply on Him, and allowing Him room to work and move in my life.

(Since writing this book, through much research and experimentation, I came to understand how to manage my FMS more effectively, and to live and eat in a way that is most beneficial for my specific needs. As a result my condition dramatically improved and I have enjoyed a great change in my quality of life. More on this recovery will be available in an upcoming book on overcoming fibromyalgia.)

While I have written much in this book about the blessings that can be gained from illness, yet it is equally true that to resign ourselves to suffering is to rob ourselves of a great blessing—the chance to feel a miracle at work in our lives. While God is able to bring good out of our suffering, that doesn't mean that it is His will for you to suffer.

Don't suffer longer than you need to. Seek the Lord about your situation. See if He has some miracle of Grace waiting for you! Reach out by faith, and receive all that God has for you!

Chapter Thirteen

TREASURES OF DARKNESS

The divine grace and comfort I have spoken of throughout my story comes in many different ways. In this chapter, I will tell you about several unique supernatural experiences which were given to me as a touch of His Grace. Through experiences such as these, I have come to understand, in my small human way, a glimpse of His limitless and eternal love.

When I look back at each of the supernatural experiences, revelations or visions that I have had, I see that they have most often come in the most difficult and trying times, when my patience and endurance are tested to the limit. I feel as though I have gone down into the deepest and darkest caves of suffering and come out with the rarest jewels, beyond compare. *"I will give you the treasures of darkness, riches stored in secret places"* (Isaiah 45:3).

Many times, as soon as the treasure is gained, the message received and the chapter about it is written, the pain fades away, and I come out of the cave into the sunlight. I feel privileged that God has trusted me with such experiences. I know it is not for my sake alone that I go through these things. I do believe that these treasures are meant to be for you. I pray that you will find in them the strength, hope and courage to fight on in your hour of need.

If you are tempted to think that the following stories are just the foolish daydreams of a sick woman, think again. Science with all its knowledge and experience cannot invent any magic pills for peace—true inner peace that transcends circumstances. There is no potion for a soul lost in despair and hopelessness, no tonic for a spirit crushed under the weight of an unnamed burden.

Though words do not suffice me to describe what I have seen and felt, this one thing I do know: that when a life so ravaged by pain and weighted by suffering can be transformed in an instant to fly in the heavenly realm, this can only be a miracle. By sharing a few of these experiences with you, it is my hope that the profound truths contained therein may shed some light on the beauty, compassion and love of our great God.

Riding the Wings of the Wind

"Fall! Just trust Me and fall." The gentle voice whispered to my heart...

When I was a child we used to play a game in which we would dare each other to stand straight as a board and then try to fall backward into the strong arms of an adult who was waiting to catch us. It's strange, but no matter how many times I'd seen it done or tried to do it myself, it was still difficult to keep from bending my knees or doing something else at the last split second to try to break my fall. Not chickening out took a certain "letting go" that went contrary to my reasoning and reflexes. It took complete trust in the one who was catching me.

Circumstances had been so difficult, as the months of severe pain and debilitating fatigue were taking their toll. I was at a particularly low time, tired of the struggle, feeling no strength in me to fight on. It was then that something extraordinary happened. It felt as though I was really there, similar to what one would experience in a dream, but I was not at all asleep; only allowed, for a moment, to see the world from a different perspective.

I found myself standing amidst a billowing storm, atop a high mountain, as strong winds beat against me. I felt the struggles of my life surging around me. It was then that I heard the gentle voice calling out to me....

"Fall! Just trust Me and fall. Fall backwards into My arms with complete trust, like the game you played as a child."

I opened my arms outstretched, took a deep breath, leaned back, and fell.—Total abandonment, total surrender, and total trust. Slowly I fell out of the realm of trouble and storm. I fell into God! I felt the soft landing envelope me with love. I had not landed on any object of shape or form. I found myself floating in beautiful, dark, stillness dotted by tiny stars. I would call it space, but this place was not empty. It was alive, and the very nature of it filled me with courage and faith.

I felt it lift me up, high above the mountains. I felt a fresh, cool wind blow in my face. Riding on the wings of the wind, I was flying! The view was breathtaking as the mountains and valleys gracefully passed below me. I thought of the Bible verse, *"Those who hope in the Lord will renew their strength; they will soar on wings like eagles"* (Isaiah 40:31). Then I heard His voice speak again:

"This is your place of freedom! When your body is held captive on a bed of suffering, let your spirit fly. Just fall. Fall on Me. Let yourself go, and fly."

Basking in the thrill of the experience and revived by the feel of the wind on my face, I felt my joy return and my spirit receive new strength. It was refreshing and invigorating. I had learned to completely let go and fall, not onto, but into the everlasting arms, only then to be carried away by them.

This was a wonderful experience which had a profound effect on me. Though my outward condition remained unchanged, inwardly a definite transformation had come over me. My joy was full and my strength renewed. It was as though I had been healed.—Healed of a crushing burden more difficult to bear than pain itself. I had felt imprisoned by my own body, trapped within my circumstances. Yet in that place, that heavenly realm, I found true freedom in God's spirit. I could fly.

A Journey through the Tunnel

I'd heard the saying countless times. "There's always a light at the end of the tunnel." This metaphorical tunnel represents a dark place of uncertainty, fear, pain and deep sorrow, found in the most difficult times of life. I am no stranger to this tunnel, having made several long and formidable journeys there. But something happened to me that radically changed my perception. I found it instead to be a place of wonder and beauty—one of the most treasured places in my life.

It started during the time when I had cancer. I was filled with questions, uncertainties and fears. I had tried so hard to be strong and cheerful for the sake of my husband and children. Daniel was still quite weak from his own health condition. Now I was going from one surgery to another. I tried to trust, but at times the darkness and despair overwhelmed me. I came to a point of great desperation and cried out to the Lord to help me see the light at the end of the tunnel.

The answer came to me in the form of a vision. I found myself walking in the pitch blackness. I knew that this was the Tunnel of Difficulty in which I was now traveling. I could not see anything around me. I felt a hand holding mine, and I knew it was Jesus. Yet even though I knew He was leading me, I was still cautiously, fearfully, inching along with one hand in front of me, feeling for any objects I might bump into. With my feet I was careful and timid, feeling my way, slowly putting one foot in front of the other.

I heard His voice say, *"Can't you trust Me?"*

I knew in my heart what I had to do. Surely He could see the way ahead and was able to lead me on safely. I had to trust Him completely. So, I put down my hand of caution, determinedly picked up my pace a little, and walked forward. My steps became steadier. Slowly I felt my confidence building as I walked on a little faster.

Gradually, a transformation was taking place in my heart and mind. My fear was being replaced by an unshakable confidence in the One who was guiding me. It no longer mattered if I could see or not. It was a journey we were taking together, and He would not let me fall. By the end of the vision, I was running—through the black of the Tunnel. This full assurance of faith shining in my heart was as bright as any light.

Though this vision only lasted a few minutes, it had changed my whole outlook. I was running fearlessly! The light at the end of the Tunnel didn't matter so much to me anymore. I had found my peace right there in the darkness. This vision was just what I needed to sustain me through the difficult months following, until eventually the Tunnel did end. The sun broke through and God blessed our small family with a time of peace and joy.

Several years later, circumstances once again brought me to a dark and difficult time, during the long, lonely months of my illness. One day as I lay in my bed unable to move, listening to sweet music of praise, I found myself drifting down the familiar darkness of the Tunnel. I had now grown more comfortable there, as I strolled along talking with Jesus, my friend and guide. He knew I was weary of the journey. The road had been long and hard lately, and I felt tired and in need of His love and strength.

My companion stopped walking, put His arms around me, and said:

"Come now, let's stop for a while and rest. You have walked long on the road of faith. I am proud of you. Now, just let Me hold you for a while, and rest."

I felt His sweet arms surrounding me, and I lay my head on His comforting shoulder. Oh, sweet relief that filled my senses as I stood nestled in my Savior's arms. His comfort washed over me and filled me with sweet joy.

Then as we stood in the dark stillness, a beautiful, soft beam of light shone down around us, illuminating us in contrast to the darkness, and we began to dance. All time seemed to fade away as we danced with slow and gentle rhythm. Such strength and power could be found in Him, yet He was so gentle and comforting. It seemed such a sweet reward during this time of suffering. The pain was gone for a time, melted away by the comfort of His presence. Truly, I felt richly blessed.

After we had danced for some time in the soft spot light, something astonishing happened. The entire space was suddenly filled with bright light that filled everything with joy and brilliance. I saw then that we were no longer in the dark hollow of the tunnel, but we had come to a large open space, much like a train coming out of the subway tunnel and arriving at a large, brightly lit station.

The music stepped up to a lively, joyful song of praise as my Lord and I danced in the fullness of His joy. The experience was exhilarating and refreshing beyond words. I was aware of many beings and angels there, watching and rejoicing, filling the air with praise. It was an exuberant and joyful celebration of love.

Then, as the music ended, slowly the lights dimmed, and we continued once again on our journey through the dark stillness of the tunnel. When I returned to reality, I felt like a new person. Still lying there, helpless on my bed, I had received a touch of the divine.

I had been weary, discouraged and feeling heavily the weight of my affliction. But now my heart was bursting with joy and gratitude. This exhilarating experience had renewed and refreshed me on the deepest level. Tears filled my eyes as humble appreciation and wonder filled my heart. I had danced with my Lord! His comfort and peace was so real to me that no physical circumstances could shake my faith in His unfailing love.

Friend, if you find yourself stumbling in the cold dark sorrows of the tunnel, hear my voice as it echoes back to you through the long dark chamber: You need not walk it alone. Hold the hand of the guide beside you. He will lead you safely through. The way is dark, I know, but He won't let you fall. And in your time of deepest sorrow, you will find Him to be your dearest and nearest friend, waiting to give you all the strength you need to carry on.

Comforting thought: A tunnel always leads somewhere. It is not a stopping place, not a destination. It is a shortcut through the mountain of life's obstacles. And remember, no matter how long and dark the tunnel, the sun is still shining on the outside.

Friends Forever

The vision only lasted a few seconds but it left an impression that I could not forget. I had been talking to a friend, when suddenly, in a flash, I saw what I perceived to be a vision of the future. I saw myself talking with this friend in Heaven, laughing and talking about our past days on earth and all that we had experienced. This has happened to me several times now, sometimes with a close friend and once with someone I just met.

Each time, the feeling is profound. I suddenly feel as though my relationship with that person is much deeper, more meaningful, and longer lasting than the earthly friendships we have now. I feel as though I am gaining a greater understanding that there is more to life than what we see here; that our lives are destined to touch each other far into the future.

Somehow this thought is very comforting to me. Perhaps it is because I've been somewhat lonely and isolated in my present situation. I used to be highly social, with many friends. Friendships have always meant a lot to me. But fibromyalgia has a way of making even the most social person into a recluse. I am almost always too sick to go out, go to church, visit anyone or attend parties, and often too sick to even call and talk to friends. Then what do you talk about anyways, when you live in an isolated world?

Then there were also the precious friends, co-workers, and people whom I had helped and prayed for in the course of my years of volunteer work before I got sick. Did they even remember me now? Did my friendship mean anything to them anymore? What was it all for anyways, I had mused, as I lay alone in a dark room.

Over the years I gradually lost contact with all but a handful of friends, and even those I rarely spoke with. I think this seclusion and loneliness must be a common thread among those who are chronically ill.

Yet slowly, through these series of little visions, I have realized that this life is only a brief moment in time. Someday we shall all be together in heavenly bliss. Then we will share the stories and the friendships together again, in a perfect world with no more parting, sorrow or pain.

Then we will see face to face and understand heart to heart. Then I will see all the dear friends again that I miss so much. Like a high school reunion, they will not have forgotten me. We will reminisce on old times, and go on to experience a whole new world together.

Then I will also meet you, dear reader, whose name and life story I don't yet know, but whom I have prayed for many times. I think we'll find we have a lot in common. We may have had very different lives, but we both have bravely faced the hardships of this world. We have been buffeted and knocked down many times, but we'll be there to tell the story.

I look at you with high regard and admiration for your valiant fight. Like me, you may feel battle-weary and discouraged at times, but remember, even Jesus struggled under the weight of His cross, and had to be helped by a passer-by (Luke 23:26). He has great understanding of those who find the cross of their suffering too heavy to bear. He doesn't think any less of you for the tears that you cry. Nor do I.

Someday I will meet you, and we will cry tears of joy together, as our heartaches will be over. And if I find on that day that my story gave you a little strength, or fitted you with a little hope on the course of your journey, then my joy will be full. I will know it was worth it all. All the loneliness now will someday bring to me many friends, and those friendships will last forever.

Chapter Fourteen

BEAUTIFUL MESS

Why does God allow all this suffering? I sometimes found myself asking. *Surely this wasn't supposed to happen. Where did I go wrong? Can anything good come out of the mess that is my life?* When I was stuck in the middle of it, surrounded by confusion and pain, it didn't seem to make any sense at all. But little by little, as the broken pieces of my life came together, I saw that out of this mess God was making a masterpiece, worked together with love and care.

When I was a child I remember walking along the paths of the local sports center. I used to laugh and point at their pitiful bushes lining the walkways. Purchased at the same time as ours, from the same nursery, theirs were small and bare, never growing over two feet tall. Yet our bushes grew huge and plush, with beautiful shades of green and purple. If we did not trim them regularly they would be well over our heads and fully overgrow the walking paths.

Amused at their bewildered gardener, I knew the secret. We had many animals on our little village farm, animals which produced endless amounts of foul smelling 'muck'. The muck was removed from the pens every day and collected in wicker baskets at the far end of the farm. Then every so often we would have what we called a 'muck-out'.

All the baskets were loaded onto a wagon pulled by our stubborn donkey and hauled to a nearby field, where a very large pit served as a compost heap. There it had to be unloaded before returning for another load. The muck-out was a hard and dirty job, taking many hours of work. The baskets often split open. One time the whole donkey cart tipped over spilling its smelly load. Yet those are fun memories for me, as I enjoyed the rare occasion of being able to help my brothers with the dirty work.

It's hard to imagine that such gross and messy muck could become the rich, life giving compost which was the secret to our beautiful gardens. Eventually others wanted to purchase our fertilizer, and the local plant nursery would give us free plants in exchange for it.

I look at my life now, as full and vibrant in growth and color as those beautiful bushes of my youth, and I smile again because I know the secret. The pains and hardships have been as abundant as the muck at a muck-out. We wonder how anything good could come from such a mess. Yet give it some time and a change takes place. Smelly muck turns into rich fertilizer, changing the small seedlings of our lives into a plush and beautiful garden.

Get Out of the Muck

I must warn you here that hardships do not automatically equal blessings. If I take a load of that muck and start spreading it around the garden, I'd quite literally just be in a lot of sh*t. Muck is foul, it smells, it has seemingly no redeeming qualities. But after it has passed through the process of decomposition, the smell is gone, and what you have left is rich life giving nutrients to feed the soil.

God does not want you to be defeated by your circumstances. Living passively beaten down by our sufferings is to live in the muck. There is no beauty there, no rich life overflowing with goodness. There is only pain and misery. I do not believe in taking a passive approach to suffering. If I had allowed myself to wallow in my depression and accept my defeat, my story would have been quite different. I believed that God had more for me.

Too many people live in defeat and sorrow because they have accepted their state, feeling that this is their lot in life. *Things never work out for me. Nothing ever changes.* This is a dangerous mentality to have. Defeat breads more defeat, till you're caught in an endless cycle of misery.

Common too is the thinking that suffering is good for us, a thread which also runs deep in some religions. The afflicted person may accept their suffering because of a belief that it will bring them future benefit, in this life or the next. While there is clearly much good to be gained from suffering, suffering is not the goal; it is not good in itself.

Others submissively accept their suffering because they believe they deserve it. They feel that God is punishing them. I've heard some say that it is bad Karma left over from sins of a previous life, to be endured patiently. Perhaps some carry on their conscience the weight of some sin, and view their suffering as a form of penance. Yet even if this is the case, God is a merciful God; He wants to restore you. He says, *"With a little wrath I hid My face from you for a moment; but with everlasting kindness I will have mercy on you."* (Isaiah 54:8).

When I read the Bible I have never once found a place where Jesus told anyone who came to him for help, "It is God's will for you to suffer. Endure it patiently and your reward will be greater." Or, "You deserve this affliction. I will not heal you because by your suffering you will pay for your own sin." Instead I find that He first tells the man lying paralyzed on a cot. *"Your sins are forgiven."* Then He adds, *"Rise, take up your bed and walk."* (Mark 2:5, 11)

Jesus is daily telling us to 'Rise'. Rise up out of the misery and the muck and receive all the goodness of God.

Paul said, *"We are hard pressed on every side, yet not crushed; perplexed, but not in despair; persecuted, but not abandoned; struck down, but not destroyed. Therefore we do not lose heart. Though outwardly we are wasting away, yet inwardly we are being renewed day by day."* (2 Corinthians 4: 8-9, 16). These do not sound like the statements of a defeated man.

The troubles of life may weigh on us, but with God's help we can overcome. God wants you to be happy and victorious. He wants your life to be blessed. The Bible tells us, "Be not weary and faint in your mind." Don't lose hope. At some point that crawling caterpillar is destined to fly.

As a child I did not know God's love in this way. I grew up believing that if bad things happened, God must be punishing me for something. If I got sick or hurt I would pray and ask God what I had done wrong. If I messed up or made a mistake, I'd be looking around fearfully expecting something bad to happen. I automatically equated trouble with God's wrath.

Then something happened that taught me otherwise. I was fifteen years old. I lay in a hospital bed waiting to go in for a surgery. I had already rehearsed in my mind every wrong thing I'd done, and prayed for forgiveness for anything I could think of. As I lay in that bed I remember an overwhelming feeling of love. I felt a Divine presence right beside me, comforting me. I was amazed at such a pure and powerful love. I knew right then, as if I heard a voice in my heart, that this illness was not the result of any sin. God was not punishing me. He was loving me.

This surgery was probably the worst thing yet to come into my young life. Yet here when I would judge myself the hardest, God did not judge me. Instead He revealed Himself to me and told me I was loved. It was as though I was meeting God for the first time.

That experience had a profound effect on me. In the days and weeks after this, I would sit out on my balcony every night and talk to God. I cried a lot out there under the starry sky, mostly tears of joy. Knowing how much He loved me gave me faith to trust my life to Him.

It is sad to see so many people caught in this trap, unable to see and receive the Lord's love because they live in fear of Him. Even after this experience I continued to carry those misconceptions of God for many more years. Coming from a strict religious background, it had been second nature to me to judge myself constantly, trying to measure up to a standard of perfection I could never reach. It would take years of God's patient pursuit of me before I could finally understand the height, depth and breadth of His love.

I knew there would be people who would look at our seeming endless stream of troubles which I have written about and judge us critically. Surely we must have strayed out of God's will or sinned big time for God to be dealing with us so harshly. In this line of thinking there is a tendency to over-spiritualize everything—to forget that hardships, pain and suffering are a natural part of human life.

We live in an imperfect world. It is not until we get to Heaven that we will ever truly be free from these weights and enjoy the beauty of God's perfection. But until that day comes I will embrace the challenges life sends my way, learn all I can from them and allow God to use them to make me into a stronger and more compassionate person.

You're Stronger than You Think

Look at the great men and women of history, and you will see countless amazing stories of enduring strength, perfected by trying ordeals. These are the stories I look to for courage in my times of testing. In a life so beset by hardships, what is it that makes men find greatness? On closer inspection we find that most often ordinary men were made great by extra ordinary circumstances. They allowed their adversities to make them strong. They did not give up and complain about their misery. Instead they used their stumbling blocks as stepping stones. They took on the challenges of life with pride.

I know all too well, that when hardships have held you down for so long, it's easy to get weary with the extended battles and multiple defeats. There were times when I felt like; *I just can't bear it any longer. The pain and pressure are more than I can endure. I can't take it one more day.* But amazingly enough, the next day came and passed, followed by another day, and another. And what do you know, I'm still here! I have survived and can now look back amazed at how far I've come. I wanted to give up, but I couldn't. As a result I am *forced* to discover that I am stronger than I thought I was.

People have sometimes said to us, "Your story is such an encouragement to me. Whenever I feel overwhelmed by my troubles, I remember all that you've been through and how strong and brave you are. This gives me courage to keep fighting on."

When I hear this I don't know whether to laugh or cry. "I don't feel strong or brave." I reply. "I'm struggling to keep my head above water, barely surviving."

To which I hear. "Yes, but look at what you're up against. Anyone who can survive under such circumstances is pretty amazing."

You too may feel like you are being beaten down time and time again. But look at the size of your opponent! You are in the boxing ring with a foe three times your strength and body weight. You are a hero just for holding your ground and making it this far. You may be wounded and weary, but look how far you've come. You're still here. So stand up tall and hold your head up with pride. Realize how strong you really are. Someday others may look to you for courage, and find strength in your story.

Take on each day as a challenge for greatness, even if your only accomplishment is to survive the strong headwinds blowing against you. You are climbing the high alps of adversity. It's hard, cold, and lonely. But climb on. Forge ahead against the winds, defy the elements. Get to the top and boldly drive in your stake and place your flag, to show yourself and the world that you made it. You are a winner. You didn't give up.

I will admit that there are times when things seem hopeless. When it seems all the cards are stacked against you. All visible means of help has failed you. Times when you feel you have fought bravely and tried everything, but you still aren't getting anywhere. Maybe you feel the burden *really* is too heavy. Maybe the hole you're in is too deep for you to get out of yourself. Perhaps you simply cannot do it on your own and need a helping hand. Call out to God for a touch of miracle to give you that extra edge, that push in the right direction.

When I find myself trapped by my surroundings, and if prayers for relief do not bring about the changes I am looking for, I focus my prayers a new direction. I pray, "Jesus, walk with me through this day. Be here by my side at every moment, and give me the strength to face the challenges today brings. Let your presence be the light in my darkness. Touch this day with a miracle."

Every new day brings with it the chance for a miracle. No matter how bad yesterday was, how bad you felt, or how much you failed, today is a new day. The Bible tells us that God's mercy is renewed every morning. (Lamentations 3:22,23) When you feel that you have used up your store of grace, and your strength has all run out, don't neglect to go to Him to be refilled again and receive His love and mercy for another day. He never runs out. He never gets tired of you. He gives, and gives, and gives again.

Your circumstances may have closed in around you, but they cannot control who you are on the inside. You have the inborn resilience of the human soul; combine that with the divine strength that comes through depending deeply on God, and you have an unbeatable combination. God's power within you is greater than all that that the world can throw against you. As the saying goes, "There is a power to lift you up that is stronger than all the powers that hold you down."

Following are lyrics to a song I wrote. I wanted to add this because there are times when we need to stand strong and remind ourselves that our problems do not define us. So stand up boldly and smile. Shake your fist at the wind and loudly proclaim your victory. You are a lot stronger than you think you are. With God on your side, *nothing* can defeat you.

Come What May

My steps may be slow, but I'll keep moving on.
My voice may be weak, but it sings a sweet song.
My way may be dark, I may feel afraid.
My knees may be knocking, but it can't shake my faith.
I may be alone and have no help in sight,
But I know You are with me. It'll all turn out right.

I just want you to know, Lord, that I'll be OK,
Just as long as you hold me each step of my way.
Come what may.

When storm billows roar, and waves mount up high,
Lead me to the Rock that is higher than I.
I'll stand on that Rock and sing over the wind,
"Fierce storm hold your fury, I'm trusting in Him
You can thunder and blow, but I will stand secure.
I know nothing can move me. My foundation is sure."

I just want you to know, Lord, that I'll be OK,
Just as long as you hold me each step of my way.

Come what may.

I won't give up the faith.

Cause your blessed assurance,

Is what gives me indurance.

So, come what may.

Marie Morrow

Chapter Fifteen

FINDING THE BEAUTY IN LIFE

When life is difficult and pain and stress threaten to block the joy out of our lives, it is especially important to look for the beauty around you. This is a concept so simple it almost seems like poetic rambling. Yet this has often been my sanity saver when the circumstances around me seemed so bleak and overwhelming. If we get our eyes too close to the trees in front of us, we forget the beauty of the whole forest. God has made so much that is good in life; we just need to look for it.

I have learned that when I make an effort to see God's love in different situations, or in the people around me, I find treasures and blessings hidden in the most unexpected places. I see His smile shining on me in the warm sunshine. I feel the gentle touch of His love in the breeze on my face. I receive His words of encouragement from my little child. One little flower can seem to warm its way into my heart, or a brilliant rainbow can renew my faith in His promises.

He is speaking to you. The voice of His love echoes from every tree. He is daily reaching out to touch you through things in your daily life. If you are able, take a walk in the sunshine, or sit on a chair in a garden, just soaking in God's presence. Even beautiful pictures in your room or a vase of flowers on the table can have a soothing effect, if you take the time to really look at them and meditate on the beauty therein.

In the bright and busy days of my strength these small blessings of life had previously missed my notice. But in the dark of my night I was amazed to discover the beauty of the stars. God's creation is the work of His hands. It is in them that we see His face.

The Colors of Life

Why are the trees such a brilliant green?
And why is the rose so deep red?
Why is the tapestry of all of life,
Woven with such colored thread?

The unblemished white of the lily and clouds,
The sky and the sea so bright blue,
The colors of spring paint so cheerful a song,
The rainbow exhibits its hue.

Even the dark of the darkest night,
Holds color in its unique way,
Enriching the contrast of darkness and light,
Enhancing this perfect display.

God could have created the world a dark drab,
Simple and colorless, plain.
Color will not help the flowers to grow,
Or sweeten the songbird's refrain.

But God has created this world for us all,
And kissed it with color and flare,
So that we could see the kind face of His love,
Reflected in all we see there.

So stop for a moment to take in the view,
To bask in the sun's golden glow.
Let Him shine His rays deep through to your heart,
That all of His love you may know.

Marie Morrow

"For the invisible things of Him from the creation of the world are clearly seen, being understood by the things that are made" (Romans 1:20a KJV).

The beautiful sun shines hot and bright 365 days out of the year. Yet how often do we take the time to notice? When's the last time you thought, "Wow, look! The sun is shining today. God must love me." Yet despite our apparent lack of appreciation, the sun continues to shine each day, providing food, heat, gravity, and all that is needed to support life. Likewise the light of God's love shines on us every day, surrounding our lives with warmth and beauty.

On the contrast however, one bright moon on a dark night seems to attract a lot more attention. My kids will say, "Wow! Look at the moon." It peeks out from behind a cloud and we take notice. Is it not true in much of life? The daily joys and beauties that surround us barely catch our notice. But the light that shines through the darkness captivates our hearts.

God's love is always shining, in the day and in the night, 365 days a year. Don't forget to look. Step out into the sunshine and let God's light smile on you.

There is Joy

There is joy to be found today.

There is beauty to be seen today.

Though your heart feels dark and cold,

Depression's grip has taken its hold.

Just open your eyes and look around.

There's a blessing to be found.

A little cheer to ease your pain,

A little drop of refreshing rain,

A little scent from a fragrant rose,

A little word that says He knows.

Dear one whose world is dark and bleak,

It's a beautiful world if you take a peek.

One little smile, one simple song,

A ray of hope when the days are long;

Just look today to find one thing,

One reason to smile, one song to sing.

One joy each day, it's a simple start,

To let the light back into your heart.

Marie Morrow

God also wants to show us His love through the people around us. But we need to let down our walls in order to receive the Love that He wants to show us through the people in our lives. We are the hands through which Christ can reach out to touch another. This is a two-way street.

First, be open to receive His love through the people around you. Relax. Enjoy those who are the closest to you. Smile now and then. Let the stress melt away for a moment, and really connect with someone. Teach yourself to recognize and appreciate those little times when friendships are shared. It's easy to let stress steal away your joy, and rob you of the support that you need the most.

Secondly, let Jesus reach through you to touch another life. There is great joy to be found in giving, and as you get your mind off yourself and reach out to someone in need, you will find the blessing returned upon you. You can never out-give God. It doesn't have to be some big charity project. Most of the time, it will be the little acts of kindness, shown in your everyday life, that will make the difference.

Illness is very stressful on everyone in the family. They may not show it in the same way, but it takes a toll. Tensions rise and relationships are strained. That is when the little things count the most. Make an effort to be kind and gentle when you are tempted to be grouchy and short-tempered. I know all too well how difficult this can be when you are tired or in pain, but it pays off. A little smile, or a thank you, or an "I'm proud of you" can go a long way. A few minutes with your child can not only assure him or her of your love, but can also go a long way to fill your own "love cup" as well! Invest in the relationships around you, because in the end, that is what really matters the most. None of us can really know how much time we have left...

The Miracle in the Music

How is it possible to stay positive, and have joyful spiritual experiences, while in the midst of severe suffering? At times like this, it would seem nearly impossible to focus on anything other than the pain and weariness. I discovered a special miracle that had the power to lift me above my earthly circumstances, and bring me into intimate communion with my Savior. It is the miracle power of music.

Music has healing power: it can soothe, calm and relax, but that's only the start of it. Good music can be a conduit for the Spirit of God. Just as electricity travels easily through water, so the Spirit of God flows through music of praise that comes from the heart. It can fill your room, your heart and your life with His presence.

It definitely matters what kind of music. When I was in pain, I was especially sensitive. If a song rubbed me the wrong way, was too fast, or had too much of a beat, it would actually increase my pain. Some songs would make me think more about my troubles and drag me down, but the right music could change my bed of suffering into a sacred place of fellowship with Heaven. This has been my most significant source of strength throughout my times of illness.

My memories of these times are many and sweet. It is a deep inner strength that cannot be described; it must be felt. The songs I loved expressed the true feelings of my heart. They were songs of sweet praise shining through a broken heart that was fully trusting in God. This was where the power and peace came from.

The great King David discovered this power. David's life was filled with many difficulties and hardships. His Psalms expressed the distress of his heart, yet lifted his thoughts to God's love and greatness. To this day, his Psalms and songs of suffering and praise are loved and sung by Christians the world over.

This is the music that became my joy, my connection to Heaven. I have compiled some of my favorite music on my website, Marie'sReflections.com. Feel free to find what works for you, and see for yourself how helpful and therapeutic music can be.

Chapter Sixteen

EMBRACE THE LIGHT

I was speaking last night with a friend whose father is dying of cancer. The doctors have given up hope and told him he has only a short time left to live. As I was on my way home my heart was deeply burdened for this friend. I thought about the many cases where God has intervened and done miracles that are humanly impossible. I do hope and pray that he can have such a miracle. But what about the many cases where God doesn't heal?

What would I say to a person who is terminally ill and knows they don't have much time left? I can hardly begin to imagine the wide range of feelings, emotions and fears that are very real at a time like that. What could I say to the person preparing to make the transition from this life to the next, leaving behind family, loved ones, and all that is familiar? How could I make his road easier?

You may have lost a loved one, friend, parent or child, or perhaps you, or someone you know, is now facing the *valley of the shadow of death* personally. Death touches everyone's life at one time or another.

I have not been to Heaven myself, but I *can* speak about what I *have* experienced personally. *I have met Jesus.* I have spoken with Him, heard His voice, and felt the comfort of His loving arms. I know that He will be there waiting to receive me, and I am not afraid to embrace the Light when it calls me.

I have a friend who had never left the United States. He was preparing to make a trip to Taiwan to visit us, and together with our family, we would travel to China. This would be an exciting adventure for all of us. This friend had told me, "I would never dream of taking this trip, if I were not going with someone I know, who already knows the country and the people. It will be a strange new land, new language, and everything different. The only thing I will have that is familiar to me is your family. I fully trust you to take care of everything, and lead the way."

I think I'd have to say the same about the next life. I've never been there before. It will be all new to me, but I am not afraid, because I have a friend waiting for me on the other side who will pick me up when I arrive, and take me to my new home. I fully trust Jesus to take care of everything, and lead the way. He has planned every detail and made every arrangement. Knowing that He will be with me, I can look forward with joy and anticipation to the adventure we will take together.

I had to come to terms with my own feelings on the subject of death, as we battled with my husband's life-threatening illnesses for many years. I really did not know how much more time we would have together. Often it seemed that each night was a struggle of life and death. We found ourselves talking deeply about our feelings and beliefs on the afterlife and what we imagined Heaven would be like. I thought about the stories I had read of people who had survived Near Death Experiences and told of indescribable beauties and joys they had experienced on the Other Side. I also enjoyed reading the description of Heaven written in the Bible.

I believe that death is to leave this tired body, and be free from pain and suffering. It is to go to a place where God's love is the life force of all existence, where there is true freedom, joy and peace, greater than anything that you have ever imagined. How do I know that such a place of joy really exists? *I have experienced it!* When?— Each time when God has given me temporary relief from my suffering and allowed me to have glimpses into the wonderful joys of His spiritual realm. Some of these visions I have written about in this book, and still others are so special that I lack the words to express them.

These magical experiences have the power to lift me above my pain, and to turn my bed of suffering into a blessed haven of bliss, opening to me a window to that Heavenly world. I find it impossible to adequately describe what I have experienced. Yet, what is more important is the effect that such experiences have had on me. The glimpses that I have had into this realm fill me with a divine peace that transcends all earthly circumstances. It fills me with so much joy, that, in spite of my pain, I feel I have found the greatest treasure on earth.

Can this be real? How can someone going through the difficult road of cancer find Divine peace? Is it possible, while suffering the painful and debilitating effects of fibromyalgia, to experience supernatural joy? Is it possible to look death in the face and fear no evil? I have been there. I have experienced this in my own life. I can only explain it as a miracle of God's love.

When my time comes and I see Jesus, we will not be strangers meeting for the first time. He has shared every treasured memory with me, walked every difficult road with me, and been a part of every joy. As lovers held apart by circumstance, I have waited for the day of our joyful reunion when we shall see each other face to face. I have often wondered what that day will be like. What will I do when I finally come before Him? Will I stand in awe, transfixed by His holiness? Will I fall to His feet in humble appreciation? Or will I leap into His arms for that long awaited embrace?—Together at last!

Do you perhaps feel that you are not ready to meet Him? Do you not yet know Him as I do? Are you afraid to face the great unknown? Are there things in your life that you have not yet made right? You can talk to Him now. You can tell Him your fears and concerns. You can ask for His forgiveness for mistakes you have made. You can tell Him that you want to receive His love. Jesus offers you total forgiveness and total love. It is not free, it cost Him His life; but He gives it to you freely because He loves you.

It is never too late to receive Him. Even when Jesus was dying on the cross, there was a thief being executed alongside Him. As he was dying, this thief acknowledged Jesus as his Savior and said, *"Jesus, remember me when you come into your kingdom." Jesus answered him, "I tell you the truth, today you will be with me in paradise"* (Luke 23: 42, 43). Three days later Jesus rose from the dead, in order that "By *His death He might destroy him who holds the power of death; that is the devil"* (Hebrews 2:14).

A Glimpse of Heaven

Before His death, Jesus told His disciples, *"Let not your heart be troubled; you believe in God, believe also in Me. In My Father's house are many mansions... I go to prepare a place for you. And if I go and prepare a place for you, I will come again and receive you to Myself; that where I am, there you may be also. And where I go you know, and the way you know."*

Thomas said to Him, "Lord, we do not know where You are going, and how can we know the way?"

Jesus said to him, "I am the way, the truth, and the life. No one comes to the Father except through Me." (John 14:1-6 NKJV)

What is this place He has prepared for us? What is Heaven like? This beautiful description of Heaven is found in Revelations chapters 21 and 22.

Re. 21:4 He (God) will wipe every tear from their eyes. There will be no more death or mourning or crying or pain, for the old order of things has passed away.

Re. 21:18,19 The wall was made of jasper, and the city of pure gold, as pure as glass. The foundations of the city walls were decorated with every kind of precious stone.

Re. 21:21 The twelve gates were twelve pearls, each gate made of a single pearl. The great street of the city was of pure gold, like transparent glass.

Re. 22:1,2 Then the angel showed me the river of the water of life, as clear as crystal, flowing from the throne of God and of the Lamb, down the middle of the great street of the city. On each side of the river stood the tree of life, bearing twelve crops of fruit, yielding its fruit every month. And the leaves of the tree are for the healing of the nations.

Re. 22:5 There will be no more night. They will not need the light of a lamp or the light of the sun, for the Lord God will give them light. And they will reign forever and ever.

Throughout the difficulties I have faced, my greatest source of comfort and strength has been the messages I have received from Jesus in my hours of need. I wish that others can know the comfort of His loving voice. I know that my own words fall sadly short of giving the help and assurance that is needed. So I tarried long in prayer on behalf of those facing the valley of the shadow of death, asking Jesus to speak to you, and receiving some words of comfort from Him to pass on to you. It is my prayer that His words can touch your heart and fill you with His peace.

"I see you there, and I know your heart. Some are afraid to come to Me, afraid of what to expect, afraid of pain, darkness, void, and all that is unknown. Come a while, and rest with me. Let me wash away all your fears in a moment of my presence. Receive my words of love, and believe in the strength that they can give you.

"I am Love. I am the fullness of Love. I am all that your heart has ever desired. Every fear can be replaced by my love. Every needy heart can be filled by my love. I am inviting you to be a part of this love, to receive all that I have to offer you. Let me fill you today to the full. Let me answer every question, and remove every fear.

"Who am I, and how do I know you personally? I am your creator. You started your life under my watchful care. You made many choices in your life, some of which brought you closer to the love that I created for you to have in your life, and some of which led you along other paths, and you have missed the strength of My loving hand. I am reaching out to you now with a hand of Love, to guide you back to Me. Let us end this race together. I will give you strength, courage, comfort, and peace to face any

test. I will hold you in My loving arms, as you take your last breath.

"I am not afraid to talk about death. It is only a passage way into My eternal kingdom. There is no fear there, no evil. There is nothing to fear if you have Me beside you. I am your protector, your redeemer, your guide, your loving father, waiting with open arms to take you home. Please don't choose to walk this road alone. Don't go unprepared.

"Perhaps you have heard of the horrors of Hell, and wonder if there is such a place. Perhaps you feel you have not yet atoned for the wrongs in your life, and wonder what the afterlife will bring. You could have shown more love, you should have been more kind. You wonder what your life is worth, and what good you have done. There is not one person who lives a perfect life. This life is filled with disappointments and failures, regrets and pains. But this is the learning ground for the truest lessons in your life. This is where your character grows. No one makes all the right choices, but we learn from the ones we make. This is life.

"I offer full atonement for all your sins, failures and shortcomings. I have pardoned it all. You cannot work for it. There is no price you can pay for it, or any rituals that can earn it. This is divine mercy, given only to those who ask for it. I have given it, but you must receive it. This is the sacrifice I made for you. My body was the price I paid for you. I died on the cross for you. Then I rose from the dead for you, to conquer death and give you eternal life with me forever. Then My joy can be full, when I receive you into My Heavenly kingdom and share My joy with you. This is the full cycle of life and death, that death could bring Eternal Life with Me.

"What is Heaven? Heaven is My home, the home for all that is good, pure, and joyful. It is a place of rest, and surcease from the pains, worries and strains of earth. It is a place of joy unspeakable (beyond words), and full of glory. It is a fulfillment of your dreams and the desires of your heart. It is a place of reward for the love that you have shown, and the good that you have done. I have seen the good you have done, and your love will be rewarded. "As much as you have done it unto the least of these My brethren, ye have done it unto Me (Mathew 25:40)."

"Your accomplishments and your money have no value here. They are worthless to me. 'Do not store up for yourselves treasures on earth, where moths and vermin destroy, and where thieves break in and steal. But store up for yourselves treasures in heaven, where moths and vermin do not destroy, and where thieves do not break in and steal. For where your treasure is, there your heart will be also.' (Mathew 6:21) The true treasures can be found in a heart that is yielded to Me, and overflowing with My love on others. Only what is done out of love will last. The rest is as ashes carried away in the wind.

"It's never too late to turn to Me. It's never too late to start over. It's never too late to say, 'I love you,' to seek forgiveness, or to give a word of kindness. It's never too late to know Me and to receive Me, to make your heart right with Me. This is the peace that I offer you. I can help you make things right in your heart and mind, with your friends and family. I can hold your hand as you take each painful step. At times it is painful, as you prepare to say 'good bye' to those you love. But I can wipe away those tears; I can give you strength to take those difficult steps. We can do it together.

"Someday the pain will be forgotten. Someday your joy will be full. On that joyful day when I call you home, then all the pain will be gone forever, the sorrow will be washed away. The love you have will never die. The friends and loved ones you leave behind will never be forgotten. They will live on in your heart and mind, until that great reunion when you can see them again. Then you will be with them forever, sharing your joy together in a perfect world where all will be made right."

Don't Die Until You're Dead

While it is a wonderful thing to have peace about the afterlife, please remember, *Don't die until you're dead!* This may sound funny or even heartless, but it has a lot of truth to it. Don't give up on life. *Where there is life, there is always hope.* Only God knows when your time will come. Doctors do not know you as well as God knows you. He may have a plan for you that you cannot see yet. There are endless stories of people who defied all medical and scientific odds, recovering from terminal illnesses, and going on to enjoy many more happy years.

Miracles do happen! Sometimes they are supernatural miracles of Divine healing. In many cases, people have found a miracle of their own in the natural remedies, foods, and supplements that God has put on this earth for our benefit. For some people, a strict exercise regimen has restored their bodies to full health, though it had seemed they were beyond hope. Even the love of friends and family, and the joy of laughter, can have a healing effect on the human body.

Who are we to say when our time will be? Life is short for all of us. The best that we can do is to make sure our hearts are right with God and others. Then we can treasure each day we have as the blessing from God that it is. Let's live each day as if we were preparing for eternity. None of us know how much time we have left. Let's love as if this were our last day to love, and then let us look forward with joy to the glory that awaits us in His Heavenly Kingdom!

Tears Turned to Gold

Chapter Seventeen

FOR THOSE LEFT BEHIND

Jesus understands the pain we feel at the loss of a loved one. When Jesus' friend Lazarus died, the Bible tells us that *"Jesus wept."* Then the people said, *"See how He loved him"* (John 11:35, 36). When He went to the tomb where Lazarus was buried, He was overcome with emotion. He was the Son of God, and knew that Lazarus would rise from the dead. Yet He was also in human flesh, and was able to experience our sorrow, and the grief that death can bring.

There is a sense of emptiness and longing; a hole has been left in our lives, and we struggle to cope with the shock of it all. We go through the motions, but something great is missing. Life can lose its joy and balance. Life has changed, and it takes time to adjust to this change. Give yourself time to heal, and to see the joy and beauty around you again. Let your loneliness press you closer to the One who fills all loneliness. He has said, *"Never will I leave you; never will I forsake you"* (Hebrews 13:5b). *"I will not leave you comfortless, I will come to you"* (John 14:18 KJV).

Besides the grief and loss of losing someone close to you, there are also very real fears and concerns that can be difficult to face. I remember mine well. "How will I raise my small children without a father? How will I support myself? What will I do? How will I make it without the loving support of my husband, which I depended on so much? Could I find it in me to go on?" I did not have the answers to these questions. I could not see the future, but I *could* trust my life into the capable hands of the One who can.

> Many things about tomorrow
> I don't seem to understand.
> But I know who holds tomorrow
> And I know who holds my hand.

I held firmly to my belief that if God allowed such a thing to happen to me, then He would provide me with the grace to endure it, and the means to go on. One thing I had seen repeatedly in my life, no matter what terrible things happened to me, God was always there to help me through it. My faith in God's love for me was unwavering. I could doubt and question anything else but this. He, who loves me so much, will not leave me abandoned and helpless. I do not claim to be strong or brave, but by looking to His love alone I could find strength.

He is a father to the fatherless, help for the helpless, strength for the weary, and comfort for the broken heart. Do you need some miracle of grace to get you through the hard times? Ask Him for it. Believe in His strong hand that can protect, love, and care for you. Let Him be your shelter from the cold winds of loneliness. Let Him fill the empty places in your life, and bring peace. Trust in His love to carry you through.

Has condemnation or guilt come in? Are you wishing for what could have been, or what you should have done differently? Were there unfinished words that should have been said, unresolved feelings that haunt you? Jesus is the Great Physician. There is no heart that He cannot heal. Receive the healing balm of His love to soothe your fears. Let His cleansing waters renew you, and wash away the pain of the past.

Ask Him to help you make things right, and give understanding to you, and even, if need be, to your departed loved one. You can trust that He loves them, and you can trust them to His loving hands. He holds the keys to the unseen world and can bridge unspoken chasms. He's the creator and master of realms; His love is their creative force.

The Rainforest

When facing such seeming tragedy, it is easy to question "Why?" Some people feel angry with God, and wonder how He could have allowed such a thing to happen. What is the good that can come of it?

I recently met a young woman, Faith Hellyer, whose mother had passed away a few years earlier, after suffering a debilitating sickness called Huntington's disease. We talked for hours about our experiences, and what we had learned from them. She told me of the hurt and confusion she felt seeing her mother suffer, the emotions and questions that clouded her heart. Then, one day, a change came over her when God spoke to her in a dream, comforting her heart and answering her unspoken questions.

He said "I bring tears into your life to water the soil of your heart; otherwise the goodness would be lost. These tears bring the richness to your life, and I allow beauty to spring forth in My good time."

Hellyer writes: In the dream, I saw that if we didn't have difficult times, our hearts would be like a desert where the sand is swept away in any direction the wind takes it. Good top soil must be moist, and thus it rains to bring forth the beauty. He brings to each of us seasons of "rain" to water the garden of our hearts.

As we spoke, she then told me about a different heartache she was recently facing that was causing her considerable distress. Then she smiled through her tear-stained face, and laughed, "I guess He's making my heart a rainforest." We smiled, as the illustration was both sad and comforting. The extended cycle of heartbreak and tears made her feel as though "it just keeps raining." Yet as we spoke I could feel that she was a special woman, filled with kindness and compassion. I could see her life as a beautiful rainforest, thick with rich and vibrant growth.

The rainforest gets its name from its almost continual rainfall year round, between 68 – 78 inches (1750 – 2000 mm) per year. This same rainfall is what accounts for the unparalleled growth of vegetation and life that thrives there. More than half of the world's species of plants and animals are found within the rainforest—over five million different species. The Canopy itself is thought by some to contain 40 percent of all plant species, and a quarter of all insect species—suggesting that half of all life on earth could be found within the leafy towers of the rainforest canopy.

The rainforest is also known as the "world's largest pharmacy" because of the many medicinal plants found there. Over half of all medications originate from the rich diversity of plant life that is so abundant there. These medicines are used to treat a large variety of ailments. The rainforest also provides us with comfort foods and fruits we love; chocolate, coffee, bananas, mangos, avocados, and papayas were all first found in the tropical rainforests.

If your life feels like a rainforest, and it seems to never stop raining, look a little closer. See if you can find some rare and priceless flowers growing there that will perfume your heart and enrich the lives of those around you. Perhaps some fruit you have harvested there will provide medicinal healing for another heart that is sick with distress.

Molly's Story

Does God really care? Is there a purpose to life's suffering? Can beautiful flowers grow from the ashes of a broken heart?

As I thought about this subject, my thoughts kept coming back to a certain family who had been a great help to me when Daniel was ill, and had helped to care for me when I had cancer. They were a happy family, with a thriving ministry. I looked up to this mother as a Godly woman with strong faith. She had a great love for children, and was happily expecting another child.

As she neared the end of her pregnancy, she discovered that the baby had a chromosome defect. This baby girl would not be able to survive outside of the womb. This baby that seemed so healthy and kicking strong inside of her mother's womb had already wormed her way into the hearts of the family. I could only imagine the heartache of knowing that they only had a short time to share with this precious little life. They could have hardened their hearts and rejected this child, in order to protect themselves from the pain of attachment and loss. But instead, they allowed the love of this little treasure sent from Heaven to enter their hearts and change them forever.

This touching letter was read at little Molly's memorial service:

"Dear Molly,

You lived such a short life, but touched so many. You were only with us for 20 minutes, but you made us all touch base with God. We know you've gone to a better place. You changed us. You made our hearts softer. You made us closer to you, and by doing so, you accomplished your short purpose in life. Your short life knit many of us together, closer than lifetime relationships, and made us feel a kinship one with another which few seldom understand. We love you, Molly, and we'll see you in the not too distant future. Amen"

As I watched this family overflowing with love, I could see the hand of God over them. Even through their heartache and pain, God had loved them. To this day, they celebrate little Molly's birthday each year with balloons and songs, and joyful talk of Heaven. I think it is wrong for us to only look for God's love in the sunshine; we must also see it in the rain. Both are sent in love for our growth.

Butterfly

I don't think that this chapter could be complete without including this very special song, written by a friend, Jerry. There was much that I admired about him. Besides being a talented musician, composer, and singer, Jerry was also a wonderful father. Having seven children did not lessen his love for each one individually. I worked closely with this family and had looked up to them with admiration.

He and his wife, Margie had a special quality, an almost tangible kindness and compassion about them that touched any who came in contact with them. Margie was one of the key influences in my life during my most impressionable years. She had this amazing ability to connect with pretty much anyone. Even with her many pressing responsibilities, she was never too busy to counsel or comfort someone in need. It seemed that no matter what I was going through, she could always understand and care.

I remember several times asking God to make me just like her. I wanted to be able to help others the way she could. The true love of Jesus seemed to be reflected in everything she did. But this deep inner beauty does not come without a cost.

Such a pure reflection of Christ comes from staying long under His care in the gentle fires of purging, till all the dross of self is burned away. After which the gold that remains is so pure, that in its reflection can be seen the face of its maker. Now I can see that the many fires of my life were in answer to this prayer.

Jerry and Margie had had their share of fire. Although they never talked about their difficulties, I knew them well. God, in His love had sent them a special child. During his two and a half years of life, he never learned to walk or talk, but Gabriel was a joy to all who knew him. He had a beautiful smile which he shared willingly with everyone. In his few short years, Gabriel had a profound impact on this family, and on all of us. He showed us God's love and joy with such simple innocence, magnified even more strongly by his frail condition. He had been born with Down's syndrome, and his tiny body struggled hard with its many frailties and multiple handicaps.

I remember the day well. We had gathered together, friends and family, to pray for this little child whose life was hanging in the balances. I was standing beside Jerry when he received the phone call from his wife at the hospital, saying that their son had just passed away. I watched him intently, wondering how he would react to this heart breaking news.

He shared with our prayer group that his child was now home in Heaven. Then he retired to the privacy of his recording studio. I do not know what took place during the hours in that room, how many tears were shed, or if he wrestled with God as to the question of "why". But the song that he wrote that day was one of the most beautiful I had ever heard and has since touched countless lives.

Butterfly

Once the night looked kindly, once the sun did shine
On you, my gentle treasure, that once on earth were mine.
Once you smiled to see me, and once I held you near;
But now my eyes are misty, my treasure's far from here.

But I'm happy because you're happy,
Because you're in Heaven, safe at last.
Trials are past, pain is over, that cocoon's no more your home,
For you, our precious Butterfly, have flown.

Thank God the race is over, Thank God the fight is done.
Together with our Savior, we fought the war and won!
With victory now behind us, I long to soon abide
In Heaven where you're waiting, Over on the Other Side.
[Angels singing:]
"He's happy Here much stronger now
And learning things so quickly. He's so alive!
He's still your son.
We'll keep him 'til you come."]

Once I held my treasure –now you're stored away;
Once I dreamed of Heaven – it's real to me today!
And though I deeply miss you, how faint my grief shall seem
When I come to join you, beyond the rainbow's gleam.

Yes, I'm happy because you're happy,
Because you're in Heaven, safe at last.
Peace and joy, love and laughter, all abound in that new
Home,

Where you, our precious Butterfly, have flown!

Tears Turned to Gold

Chapter Eighteen

PARALLEL ROADS

How can we possibly understand the mind of God? How can we answer the questions that can plague us (or judge what is fair and right) when we see some recover from illness and others continue to suffer?

I cannot answer all your questions, but perhaps my story will shed some insight...

On a fateful day in 2000, my mother received two separate life-shaking phone calls. That was the day I called my mom to tell her I had cancer. Those are the words no mother wants to hear. Yet, unbeknownst to me, my call came only hours apart from another. My brother had called from Taiwan to tell her that he had been diagnosed with cancer. Two of us, on opposite sides of the world, somehow connected by a strange hand of fate.

My brother's journey through advanced melanoma is one far too many people can relate to. The depths one goes to, the pain and sickness, the deep depression brought on by chemical reaction to the grueling treatments, and the worry for one's family when doctors are less than hopeful. My own journey of repeated surgeries and long recoveries seemed strikingly similar. Though half a world apart, we were walking parallel roads.

We had a lot in common growing up. Only one year younger than him, I was closer to him than most of my other brothers. We had since grown and married and each had four children. We had followed the same paths into missionary service and shared our love for the Chinese people, choosing to raise our families in Taiwan. My brother and I had another thing in common, an unwavering faith in the love of God. And as we each faced our valley of suffering, we would each come to know the greatness and mercy of God in our own way.

When my brother, Aaron, first decided to become a Triathlon racer, he was barely able to climb the flight of stairs from his kitchen to the bedroom. Diagnosed with stage three cancer, he had been given a fifty percent chance of survival. The long year of surgeries and treatments had left him a near invalid. The horrible effects of the immunotherapy treatments had driven him into severe depression.

With the first big race coming up, this idea certainly seemed impossible. But God is not limited. Aaron asked God for a miracle and then actively set out to lay claim to that miracle. He began training every day, gradually building his strength. This goal gave him something to strive for, renewing his vision for life, igniting within him a spark of hope.

That spark was to become a burning flame that would light the way for countless others who today look to his story for strength and courage. Not only did he succeed in covering the full course of the triathlon, but he went on to make a full recovery from cancer, competing in many races and is currently ranked as one of Taiwan's top Triathletes.

Aaron joined various sports and biking clubs and later started his own sports team called "Team Live Right." Besides participating in competitions, they travel Taiwan giving seminars to promote cancer awareness and prevention, and the need for healthy living. His miraculous story stands out as an example of faith and perseverance, and has been featured in many news and television interviews. He even wrote a book which was translated into Chinese and sold both in Taiwan and in the U.S.

I cannot tell you that I have never questioned the different turns our recoveries took. Our cancer stories had been so similar. We even had our major surgeries on the same day. But now he is a shining example of health and fitness, and I am the picture of quiet weakness. There were times I wondered why God chose to heal Aaron and not me. Did I do something wrong?

Yet, as I write this book, I see my life as perfect. What God has given me through all my experience I wouldn't trade for anything in the world. Both our books, while very different, follow the same central theme—A loving God who reaches us in our weaknesses and carries us out. He delivered my brother in the form of health and strength. Yet the deliverance He has given me in the form of spiritual healing and heavenly strength is no less miraculous. If our very different stories can, each in its own way, be a help to some struggling soul, then we will have fulfilled our purpose. God truly has given us parallel roads.

The real question to ask myself then is not why I have been dealt the cards I have in this life, but what will I do with what I have. Can I really say that one person is disadvantaged over another because of his/her disability, upbringing, past abuse or present hardships? Without doubt there are major challenges in our lives to overcome. But they do not define you! A loving God can take those very crutches, representative of your broken life, and turn them into the wings that will bear you up to your destiny.

Though I do not know all the answers, this much I do understand... A life that is fully surrendered to Christ is always a beautiful thing. "For better or for worse, for richer or poorer, in sickness and in health," that is the union we share with Him through all the long journey of life. He never promised us an easy road, but He did promise to be with us every step our road may take.

Any life that is given to Christ, no matter how broken, holds all the potential of the risen Savior—to restore, renew and bring to greatness. Be all that you can be through Him!

In Conclusion

A number of scientists, doctors and psychologists are now attesting to the remarkable healing power of one's personal faith. According to studies, a person with strong faith and a positive outlook on life has a far higher chance of beating cancer, has less chance of heart disease, and many other health benefits.

It is said that it doesn't matter what you have faith in; but it is the power of the mind that having faith itself gives you. There are many books and speakers who teach in length on this subject, praising the tenacity of the human spirit in times of crisis, and teaching you to find strength from within. Having faith in ourselves, a strong will to survive, and determination to overcome is vital in learning to triumph over life's hardships.

There is great strength to be found in mental attitude and perseverance. The human spirit is a powerful thing. In fact, you never know how strong you really are until you are pushed beyond the limits of your comfort zone. Then you see what kind of person you really are.

Yet, on the other hand, I acknowledge that there is a limit to our human strength. Our human power, as amazing as it is, has natural limitations and weaknesses. To put your faith in your own strength can only take you so far. But God's power is limitless, His strength is unending and His love and compassion reach out to us daily. To avail myself of God's help is not weakness, it is the greatest strength of all.

You see, if my faith is in God, the strong, loving, compassionate, all knowing, all powerful, all wise, King of the universe, circumstances cannot have as much power over me. He is in control of my life and that is all I need to know. If you are looking into His eyes, and trusting completely in His love, then you can never be disappointed, because He who loves you so much could never do you any wrong.

You too can experience a touch of the supernatural in your life. This is a victory and a joy that transcends all earthly circumstances and conditions. It can turn your desert of pain into an oasis of hope—and it is available to you! Jesus has the power to transform the situation around you, to illuminate it with God's presence. Once He is there with you in your circumstances, everything changes! He can fill the dark chambers of your life with His peace, and the sweet riches of His Spirit. This is a treasure so real, that someday you may find yourself thanking God for the very heartache that brought you to His side.

Friend, If you only remember one thing from my story, let it be this: God loves you more than you could ever imagine. His love is strong enough to take any trouble in your life and turn it into a blessing, and what's more, He takes pleasure in doing so. His love is infinite, divine, perfect, undaunted by our human imperfections and weaknesses.

This is the one central theme of this book. In fact, this is the very theme of my life—the unfailing love of God.

The completion of this book marks the closing of a chapter of my life. This writing process has been quite liberating for me; writing these things has helped to put closure on the events of the last seven years: painful memories have been faced and conquered, confusing memories have become clear, wonderful treasures have been recorded.

I see the pattern of God's plan as it has unfolded, and it is perfect. Now I look on to the future with faith and expectancy. I do not know what it will hold, but the One who has guided us safe this far will guide us safely on.

We may not have the strength that others have, but, in our own unique way, we can still serve God with the blessings He has given us. I pray that we can continue to minister to those in need by our websites and email correspondence, and to those the Lord brings our way. Our children also continue to reach out to the elderly and needy with their cheery voices, dances and smiles.

Our hearts desire is to return to Taiwan, to live among the Chinese we love, and to bring this message of comfort and hope to those who have not had the opportunity to hear it. How will we get there?! I believe that where God's finger points, there His hand will make a way. We cannot know the future; we can only follow one step at a time, as He leads.

We continue to hold on to our faith that God can and will deliver us, but we will not sit around waiting for it. We have seen the fulfillment of His promises towards us in ways more powerful than healing.

We have learned to enjoy the beauty of dancing in the rain.

Dance in the Rain

Don't sit around with a sorrowful frown,
And wait for the storm to refrain.
You poor hurting dear, get up off your rear.
Go out there and dance in the rain.

The water that drenches, cleans out our trenches,
Washing the old down the drain.
So sing with the flowers, enjoying the showers.
Get up and go dance in the rain.

Watching and hoping, while silently moping,
Will not make the sun shine again.
So move with the beat of the rain at your feet.
As you learn how to dance in the rain.

It's flooding the yard, but don't take it hard.
The stress will just drive you insane.
Try it and see how much fun it can be,
Dancing around in the rain.

Marie Morrow

Epilogue

A Dream Come True

Epilogue

A Dream Come True

It has now been six months since the completion of this book, yet little did I know, that the most significant chapter was yet to be written. What God has done for us in the last six months has turned our lives around. I am thrilled to be able to include the happy ending of this story.

I write this now, sitting in our beautiful new apartment on the thirteenth floor of our luxury apartment complex in sunny Taichung city, Taiwan, enjoying this dream come true. Our comfortable home provides me with the ideal atmosphere to rest and recuperate. The view from here is beautiful and refreshing, looking out over the park below and then further out over the city. My mother moved here with us, and continues to help me with the children. Two of my brothers already live in Taiwan with their families, so the kids have plenty of friends and help getting adjusted.

At the time of writing this book our goal of returning to Taiwan had seemed like a distant dream. I had written to a friend that we were the most unlikely family to ever make it back overseas, not only because of our health problems, but we were also deeply in debt due to previous hard times. Yet, in spite of all our obstacles, we had heard a definite call from the Lord to return to Taiwan. And if there is one thing we have learned from our experiences it is to trust God, that where He guides He will also make a way.

Daniel's condition had stabilized, and he was no longer receiving medical care. While my health was still a constant challenge, I had not found any help from doctors I had seen in the US. My location had little to do with my condition. I figured, if it's all the same anyways, I'd rather be in Taiwan where I am really happy.

A big challenge for me was to give up my electric wheel chair. I could not take it with me and it would do me no good there anyways, because very few places are designed to be wheelchair accessible. This was a real step of faith because although my health had improved some, I still often relied on the use of my wheelchair to get around. But that just made it all the more exciting because I would have to trust God to do the miracles I needed. I truly believed that if this was God's call, He would give me the strength.

I must admit though that when Daniel first pulled out the suitcases and said to start packing for this move to Taiwan, I thought he was getting pretty carried away. After all, it would take us at least another year to raise the needed money and to finish our preparations. Even though we had been working towards this goal for a year already, progress had been slow. But Daniel had come back from a two week preliminary trip to Taiwan filled with excitement about this move and fueled with faith for miracles.

Little did I realize what great things God would actually do. Only three months later we were flying towards the sunrise, in awe and wonder at all that had transpired so quickly. We left the US not only *debt free* but also with all the money that we needed to start out our new lives and to comfortably furnish and set up our new home. To top it all off, a friend decided to give the kids a special going-away present, each their own brand new laptops to use for their studies. To detail the many miracles that took place would literally take another book. God had been too good to us.

Getting set up took some time. It was a lot of work, moving seven people and everything we own across the world. Our initial landing spot was a beautiful house near the mountains, with a tropical fruit orchard in the back. We stayed there with my brother and his family, while we looked for our own place. Then we found it, our special little haven in the best possible location. When God does a miracle, He does it all the way. His goodness is immeasurable.

Life in Taiwan has been wonderful. The kids loved the change and adjusted quickly. They were young when we last left Taiwan so there is much for them to explore and discover that is new and interesting for them. Our children have had the opportunity to do many shows here, performing in local hospitals, prisons, drug-rehab center, senior citizens homes, and handicap centers, etc, bringing God's love and light to the needy.

Daniel has been quite well, continually sustained by an amazing miracle that keeps him going strong in spite of his growing tumor. The initial move and set up took quite a toll on my health at first, but afterwards I steadily improved, and I am now better than I have been in years, enjoying my family, actively involved in ministry, and yes, getting around without a wheelchair. To what do I accredit my outstanding recovery? Is it the weather, the food, or just being happy in the place I love? Or is it part of the blessings of God that have showered down on us in such abundance and surrounded us on every side?! Truly, we have been richly blessed.

When I look back at all that we have been through in the last few years, it seems almost hard to believe the life that I now see around me. How could I possibly have known in those darkest hours of night that the daybreak would give us such a magnificent sunrise?! With heart filled with praise, I offer to God this simple token of my gratitude...

"I love You, O Lord, my God, my strength; for You have done great things for us. You have lifted us up and delivered us, because You delighted in us.

"Sorrows and troubles surrounded us on every side. Our own strength was too weak to save us. I was broken and afflicted. I wept sore when hope was taken from me; but You were continually with me.

"Then You heard the cry of our affliction. Your mercy and your compassion was stirred up within you. You looked kindly upon us because of your great love.

"You caused our hope to bloom and filled our lives with joy. You reached down with your strong arm and saved us. Your loving-kindness showered upon me like rain, watering my thirsty heart. Gladly will I take my refuge in you, for You are my sanctuary of peace."

The Wealthy Place

Dear reader, if you are going through a time of severe testing, or through a path of fire and water, take heart. Psalms 66:12 says, *"We went through fire and water, but You brought us to a place of abundance."* I am here to tell you that this wealthy place really does exist. There is a place of rich rewards and blessing, peace and deliverance. We have been through the difficult path of fire and water, and we have made it through to the other side.

Friend, I am calling back to you now as you struggle on your own journey. I too have traveled that road myself. I have fallen on the rocky cliffs of hardship. I have lingered in the valley of despair. I have been through the dark forest of fear and traveled timidly through the black tunnel of uncertainty. I too have stumbled along the way.

But I have also seen the victorious end. I have come out into the light at the end of the tunnel. I have seen the rewards and found the treasures. I am calling back to tell you, don't be afraid. There is a happy end to all this suffering. And though the road is long, there will be resting spots along the way that will clear your vision and renew your mind.

The road is not easy, I know. But you don't have to walk it alone. God knows what you are going through and He cares. When you are tired, you can lean on Him. When the way is rocky, trust Him to keep your steps. When the water is deep, you can call on Him to lift you up. He is there, just waiting to help you.

If you are faltering in your time of testing, if you feel there is no end to your suffering, no light at the end of the tunnel, I urge you to hold on. The darkest hour is just before dawn. If we could make it through to the other side, so can you. That's not to say that all our troubles are over; we still battle with our health and the basic struggles of human life. But the dark night of our suffering has come to an end, and we are now basking in the sunrise of a beautiful new dawn.

I'm here to tell you that there is joy that comes after sorrow. No matter how bad things seem to you just now, no matter how hopeless, joy will come again. There is a new life to be had on the other side. There is a time of new beginnings. There is life after death—new life after the old has died.

A good friend once told me,

> *"God will not leave you on the fire forever. The fire may be necessary to purify the gold, but gold can hold no shape or usefulness until it is cooled. Eventually God takes us out of the fire and perfects in us His work of art."*

I am forever grateful for the purging fires of His love which have made me what I am today. I treasure every moment, every memory, and every touch of His hand. He has been with me through the fire, and He has brought me out. Our relationship is deeper, our bond inseparable. Now, together with Him, I am eager to explore this wealthy place of abundant blessings He has brought me to.

At the time of this book's publication, we have since returned to the U.S. after five wonderful years in Taiwan. For more news and updates, visit my website:

MariesReflections.com

Additional Pages

for your Comfort and

Inspiration

Tears Turned to Gold

Appendix A

HEAVEN SPEAKS

When I first set out to write this book, my hope was not only tell the story of our experiences but also to record and document the priceless messages we have received from Heaven, to preserve them for others and to pass down to another generation. I had hoped that someday when my children were grown that my book would open to them a glimpse into the secret places of my life and pass on to them this treasured heritage of faith.

These messages are significant not only for the particular guidance and encouragement that they afforded to me during my times of illness, but more importantly because in reading them I come closer to understanding the heart and mind of a loving and caring God. At times I am surprised at the candid and personal way in which He speaks, without the piety some would expect from a deity. Though He is the God of Heaven, He can be so down to earth, relating to us and our human needs.

This section contains a collection of additional personal messages received from Heaven for our situation, which are not included in the story above. These are a few of my favorites which I have recorded and saved over the years. I share them now in the hopes that others, who are perhaps weary with their own difficult journey, might also benefit from the encouragement and insight contained therein and find renewed strength to carry on.

Consider the lilies of the field, how I care for and provide for them. But you are bogged down again with many worries. Always, I need to lift you up again. Don't be afraid to come back to Me to get a new dose of My strength for the day. I am always ready to give again. When your faith is low, when your courage runs dry, when the mountains before you seem insurmountable, when your strength fails and your frame is weak, I am always there, always strong, always ready to lift up your head and smile kindly.

I do not give you more than you can bear. I am there to lift your burden and ease your pain. This comfort and relief is available to you at all times. For with this affliction, I have given you means to bear it. Believe not those lies which seek to tell you of your shame and to condemn you, as though you of yourself need do anything of yourself to be worthy of this great love, for it is given freely.

I knew these burdens would be too much for you to bear. I did not ask for you to bear them alone. You don't need to show Me how strong you are, or to demonstrate your bravery. I know you have these qualities and have shown them many times over. Now I say to you, rest when you are weary. Give Me the burdens of your heart, and see if I will not carry them better than you.

If you could know My heart, you would know I do not afflict willingly. It is hard for Me as well. I feel your pain. Have you ever thought of that?—How much it pains My heart to see you suffer? – Especially you who are so dear to Me, and who bare it so bravely in My name? This time has been a deepening for both of us—a deepening of our love, a sacrifice of untold worth.

Do not forget the sacrifice and the heartache I have had, to be up with you on those long lonely nights as you suffered bravely, clinging to Me. I was there, holding you, when you knew your own husband couldn't handle the weight of your plight. We have suffered it together, you and I. I want you to know what it cost Me, too. But now, see it from My vantage point. I see so much victory, so much glory, such great reward. I cannot wait to share with you the full reward for your labors.

You have had a different calling, and it has been hard. You have not been able to do many things which you thought you should, or wished you could. You carry the weight of blame and guilt for those many lacks. These weights are some of the heaviest you carry. But I have not asked you to carry them.

I don't see your lacks, only your victories.—Victories of drawing closer to Me, the strength you have been to others through your weakness, the sweetness of your songs and writings coming through a broken heart, your love for your children and those around you.

When it comes down to it, these are the things that count. In those things of the spirit, you are light years ahead of what you could have been, if you had continued to accomplish so much in the flesh. So do not despise your weakness, for it has worked in you a far more eternal weight of glory. I love you dearly. You are dearly loved and blessed by Me.

203

You are winners! You sometimes feel spent and worthless; I see this bringing out the best in you—and it's only the beginning. There's so much for you to gain from this time of Gethsemane. It is truly a time to treasure. If only you could grasp even a small part of what I am doing in your lives, your spirits would jump for joy!

I'm giving you a special time in My arms, a time to experience My love and get to know Me in a deeper way than you ever have before, or ever could in an easier situation. How is that not winning?

I'm giving you time to think about life, and renew your appreciation of the things that really count. As you do, the fleeting things of this Earth lose their luster and fade into the background, and the eternal things of the spirit shine more brightly and come to the fore. How is that not winning?

I'm helping you to better appreciate the love of family and friends, and vice versa. It's so easy to take each other for granted when everyone is so busy and everything is going so fast. Now you feel their love stronger than ever, and feel compelled to express your love for them more strongly than ever, and this is deepening all of you. How is that not winning?

I'm helping you put your brief life on Earth in perspective— to understand that this present world is not your destination, but a mere steppingstone to the far more wonderful world I have waiting for you. How is that not winning?

So you see, you are My brave soldiers who are real winners. As you keep your heart and mind on Me, and praise Me for all I am doing in your lives, you can't lose for winning. You'll go from victory to victory, until you pass over to be with Me. That will be the greatest and final victory, but I have many more in store for you before then. Keep your face turned up to Me, enjoy every day, every minute, every touch of My love to the full, and you will feel most richly blessed.

A Message for You

Before completing this book, I came once more before the throne of Heaven carrying a special request. I asked my friend, Jesus, if He had any message especially for you, dear reader. Following is the answer He gave me. Remember, whatever challenges you face, take shelter in His strong arms, and in Him you can find your strength.

~∿∭∿~

Reach out and take My hand, and I will walk with you all the way. All I require is a simple believing heart, and a desire to follow. Yes, you must follow if you want Me to lead you beside the green pastures and still waters. I am your guide, your friend, your helper, and your deliverer. I can be your all in all, if you will have me. I stand waiting with all that is good and needed for your life. Come and take it. Drink of My Word and be refreshed. Feed on the riches of My spirit, and be strengthened. I will fill your life to overflowing, if you just give Me a chance.

Say, 'Jesus, I want you, and all that you have to give me. I open my heart and mind to receive. I surrender my will and my life to You. Be the master of my destiny. Guide my ship over the waters of this life, and guide me safely to port.'

I will be happy to guide you. Only I, who can see from up above the maze, can tell which way for you to turn. When the road gets cold and stormy, find your shelter in Me. I will always be there for you. What looks to you like a dead end, will open out into beautiful fields and resting places. Follow closely.

I am smiling kindly upon you. My blessings are full for the taking. Reach out and receive. Receive in such great measure that you will not be able to contain it for yourself, but it will overflow on others to light their lives also. This is the blessing of the filled life. One who comes to Me often to be filled, will never go away empty. Thank you for coming to Me. It fills My heart with joy to see your tender smile, as you trust Me to care for you. How could I disappoint such trust?

So smile on. Smile through your tears. Smile in the sunshine and in the rain. Both are given in love to help you to grow.

Appendix B

GREAT AND PRECIOUS PROMISES

"Whereby are given unto us exceeding great and precious promises, that by these we might be partakers of the Divine nature" (2 Peter 1:4a KJV).

It is a wonderful joy to me that God would give such precious gifts to us as His promises in the Bible. Through His words, He is allowing us to take hold of, and appropriate for ourselves, a part of His Divine nature, His strength, love and grace. Following is a collection of some of my favorite passages of scripture. Each one is a precious treasure. They contain power and comfort to hold onto in time of need. I am including these here for your easy reference in time of need. I pray they may be a blessing to you as they have often been to me.

"Be strong and courageous. Do not be terrified; do not be discouraged, for the Lord your God will be with you wherever you go" (Joshua 1:9).

"He knows the way that I take; when he has tested me, I will come forth as gold" (Job 23:10).

"The Lord is a refuge for the oppressed, a stronghold in times of trouble" (Psalm 9:9).

"He has not despised or disdained the suffering of the afflicted one; he has not hidden his face from him but has listened to his cry for help" (Psalms 22:24).

"Even though I walk through the valley of the shadow of death, I will fear no evil, for you are with me; your rod and your staff, they comfort me" (Psalm 23:4).

"The Lord is close to the brokenhearted and saves those who are crushed in spirit. A righteous man may have many troubles, but the Lord delivers him from them all" (Psalm 34:18, 19).

"Though he stumble, he will not fall, for the Lord upholds him with his hand" (Psalm 37:24).

"I waited patiently for the Lord; he turned to me and heard my cry. He lifted me out of the slimy pit, out of the mud and mire; he set my feet on a rock and gave me a firm place to stand. Blessed is the man who makes the Lord his trust" (Psalms 40:1,2,4a).

"God is our refuge and strength, an ever-present help in trouble. Therefore we will not fear, though the earth give way and the mountains fall into the heart of the sea,

though its waters roar and foam and the mountains quake with their surging" (Psalms 46:1-3).

"When I am afraid, I will trust in you. In God I trust; I will not be afraid" (Psalms 56:3,4).

"Have mercy on me, O God, have mercy on me, for in you my soul takes refuge. I will take refuge in the shadow of your wings until the disaster has passed. I cry out to God Most High, to God, who fulfills His purpose for me. He sends from heaven and saves me... God sends his love and his faithfulness" (Psalm 57:1-3).

"I call as my heart grows faint; lead me to the rock that is higher than I" (Psalm 61:2).

"We went through fire and water, but you brought us to a place of abundance" (Psalms 66: 12).

"Though you have made me see troubles, many and bitter, you will restore my life again; from the depths of the earth you will again bring me up. You will increase my honor and comfort me once again" (Psalm 71:20, 21).

"My flesh and my heart may fail, but God is the strength of my heart and my portion forever" (Psalm 73:26).

"For he will command his angels concerning you to guard you in all your ways (Psalm 91:11).

"Unless the Lord had given me help, I would soon have dwelt in the silence of death. When I said, "My foot is *slipping," your love, O Lord, supported me. When anxiety was great within me, your consolation brought joy to my soul"* (Psalms 94:17-19).

"He will have no fear of bad news; his heart is steadfast, trusting in the Lord" (Psalms 112:7).

"My comfort in my suffering is this: Your promise preserves my life" (Psalm 119:50).

"The Lord will fulfill his purpose for me; your love, O Lord, endures forever— do not abandon the works of your hands" (Psalm 138:8a).

"O Lord... You know me. Where can I go from your Spirit? Where can I flee from your presence? If I go up to the heavens, you are there; if I make my bed in the depths, you are there. If I rise on the wings of the dawn, if I settle on the far side of the sea, even there your hand will guide me, your right hand will hold me fast. If I say, "Surely the darkness.... will hide me and the light become night around me," even the darkness will not be dark to you; the night will shine like the day, for darkness is as light to you." (Psalm 139:1,7-12).

"Thou wilt keep him in perfect peace, whose mind is stayed on thee: because he trusteth in thee" (Isaiah 26:3 KJV).

"He gives strength to the weary and increases the power of the weak. Even youths grow tired and weary, and young men stumble and fall; but those who hope in the LORD will renew their strength. They will soar on wings like eagles;

they will run and not grow weary, they will walk and not be faint" (Isaiah 40:29, 31)

"Do not fear, for I am with you; be not dismayed, for I am your God: I will strengthen you and will help you; I will uphold you with my righteous right hand" (Isaiah 41:10).

"For I am the LORD, your God, who takes hold of your right hand and says to you, Do not fear; I will help you" (Isaiah 41:13).

"When you pass through the waters, I will be with you; and when you pass through the rivers, they will not sweep over you. When you walk through the fire, you will not be burned... For I am the LORD, your God... your Savior" (Isaiah 43:2).

"I will give you the treasures of darkness, riches stored in secret places, so that you may know that I am the LORD (Isaiah 45:3).

"Though I have fallen, I will rise. Though I sit in darkness, the LORD will be my light" (Micah 7:8).

"Come to me, all you who are weary and burdened, and I will give you rest" (Mathew 11:28).

"We are hard pressed on every side, but not crushed; perplexed, but not in despair; persecuted, but not abandoned; struck down, but not destroyed. Therefore we do not lose heart. Though outwardly we are wasting away, yet inwardly we are being renewed day by day.

For our light and momentary troubles are achieving for us an eternal glory that far outweighs them all. So we fix our eyes not on what is seen, but on what is unseen. For what is seen is temporary, but what is unseen is eternal" (2 Corinthians 4: 8-9, 16-18)

"He said to me, "My grace is sufficient for you, for my power is made perfect in weakness." Therefore I will boast all the more gladly about my weaknesses, so that Christ's power may rest on me. That is why, for Christ's sake, I delight in weaknesses... in difficulties. For when I am weak, then I am strong" (2 Corinthians 12:9,10).

"For God hath not given us a spirit of fear; but of power, and of love, and of a sound mind" (2 Timothy 1:7 KJV).

"Because he himself suffered when he was tempted, he is able to help those who are being tempted" (Hebrews 2:18).

"In this you greatly rejoice, though now for a little while you may have had to suffer grief in all kinds of trials. These have come so that your faith—of greater worth than gold, which perishes even though refined by fire—may be proved genuine and may result in praise, glory and honor when Jesus Christ is revealed" (1 Peter 1:6, 7).

"Let them that suffer according to the will of God commit the keeping of their souls to Him in well doing, as unto a faithful Creator" (1 Peter 4:19 KJV).

"There is no fear in love. But perfect love drives out fear" (1 John 4:18).

Appendix C

A Prayer of Love
for Those Who Are Suffering

From my journal - March 29, 2006

Dearest Jesus,

I have so enjoyed these hours soaking in Your presence. It is such a blessed and treasured gift. How can I ever repay you, or thank you enough for the indescribable love we share between us? It is more real than any earthly love, more perfect in every way.

I was weary today, unable to find relief from such terrible pain. It would seem to be a long day of suffering, were it not for Your presence. I could not feel You there at first, but I never doubted Your presence. I suffered with patience as I held on to You.

Then I began reading this beautiful book (Within the Gates, by Rebecca Springer) describing the wondrous glories and love You have waiting for me on the Other Side. The pain faded in the beautiful thoughts and visions of Heaven and of Your splendor. Oh, my precious Jesus, I can hardly wait for that day when I will see You face to face. I shall throw my arms around You, and we shall embrace at last.

All these years You have loved me. I have failed You, and gone my own way many times, yet Your love has never wavered. My imperfect heart has erred many times, yet You have loved me all the more. Through all the years, our love has grown. First I loved You with all the purity and simplicity of a child's love for a parent. Then I learned to confide in You as a dearest friend, and yet, our love grew beyond what any earthly friendship could afford.

For You, the great King of the entire universe, have brought me near to Your own heart of love. Surly, this is the greatest love possible. Your love is intimate, personal, and free, without inhibitions or criticism, for You love me entirely as I am.

Dear Jesus, I wish that all the world could feel this love. I thank You from the bottom of my heart for this affliction, for this pain, that has brought me so near to You. It is worth it all if I can help just one struggling, suffering soul to know the freedom of Your love.

Set them free, My love. Set them free from the suffering of this world. Give them glimpses into Your Heavenly realm. Let the gifts and treasures of Your blessed presence sustain them, ease their pain, and comfort their hearts.

Don't let them suffer in vain. Help them, even now, to reach out a hand to You, to 'touch the hem of Your garment' (Luke 8:43-48) and find the healing they seek. Be real to them. Break through the barriers of our earthly realm, and let Your light flow freely into our darkened lives.

There are so many suffering. I wish I could comfort them all. You have blessed me so richly with this love, even in the midst of my suffering. Please, somehow, enable me to pass it on to those in need. Comfort them all. Let Your love shower down on them like the rain, to refresh their spirits and strengthen their hearts.

They are so brave. They have fought so well, under unimaginable circumstances. You are so proud of them. Many a crushing weight has borne down on their souls, threatening to block out the light of hope. Reach under them now, and lift their burdens. Be their strong help in time of trouble. Place a smile on their faces, and a song of praise in their hearts. Transform their suffering into a blessing in their lives, a place of growth and comfort.

I thank You that You have heard me, and that You have loved them, even as You have loved me. Give them now that peace to trust You, to believe Your Word, and rest steady on Your promises. Help Your wonderful light to overshadow the darkness. Replace fear with faith. Bring out the beauty in their lives. Bless us all with Your peace.

I am forever indebted to You, my Savior, my Friend and my Love.

—Amen

For more articles, stories,
photos and updates,
please visit me at
MariesReflections.com.

You may also contact me at:
Contact@MariesReflections.com

I would love to hear from you.

Proof

Made in the USA
Charleston, SC
20 May 2013